A BENN STUDY . DRAMA

THE NEW MERMAIDS

She Stoops to Conquer

She Stoops to Conquer

OLIVER GOLDSMITH

Edited by

TOM DAVIS

Lecturer in English
University of Birmingham

LONDON/ERNEST BENN LIMITED

NEW YORK/W. W. NORTON AND COMPANY INC.

First published in this form 1979
by Ernest Benn Limited
25 New Street Square · Fleet Street · London · EC4A 3JA
& Sovereign Way · Tonbridge · Kent · TN9 1RW

© *Ernest Benn Limited 1979*

Published in the United States of America by
W. W. Norton and Company Inc.
500 Fifth Avenue · New York · N.Y. 10036

Distributed in Canada by
The General Publishing Company Limited · Toronto

Printed in Great Britain by
Fakenham Press Limited, Fakenham, Norfolk

British Library Cataloguing in Publication Data

Goldsmith, Oliver
    She stoops to conquer. – (The new mermaids).
    I. Title   II. Davis, Tom   III. Series
    822'.6   PR3488

ISBN 0–510–34142–X
ISBN 0–393–90046–0 (U.S.A.)

FOR

MY FATHER AND MOTHER

CONTENTS

ACKNOWLEDGEMENTS

No TEXTUAL WORK ON GOLDSMITH can escape a debt to Arthur Friedman's five-volume edition (Oxford, 1966); but this text, while fully acknowledging his pioneering work, is based on a fresh collation and a different view of the textual relationships.

My personal thanks are due to colleagues and friends who have helped me in this edition. Mark Storey read the Introduction, Gerry McCarthy talked to me about farce, and Olivia Smith about politics. Wendy Davies gave me the initial impulse for the Introduction. And I have gained much from discussing the play with students at Birmingham. Any mistakes, however, are all mine.

I am, finally, grateful to my wife, who put up with a great deal.

Birmingham   T.R.D.
February 1979

INTRODUCTION

THE AUTHOR

OLIVER GOLDSMITH was born an Irishman, the second son of a not very affluent clergyman, probably in the village of Pallas, County Westmeath, probably in 1730. Soon afterwards the family moved to the village of Lissoy, one of the candidates for the role of Auburn in Goldsmith's famous pastoral *The Deserted Village*. The intensity of the longing for the idealized village of the poem is mirrored by the intensity with which Goldsmith attempted to desert his own village background: as an entrant to Trinity College, Dublin (1745); in two attempts to emigrate to America; in a flight to Dublin, intending to study law in London (both in 1750–52); finally, and successfully, as a medical student at the University of Edinburgh (1752). He stayed there two years, in considerable poverty—his extravagance not being met by his only source of income, a small allowance from his uncle—before the urge to travel took him, without a degree and after what can only have been a superficial education in medicine, for a by no means grand tour of Europe. Not much is known of his travels, except for the probably rather fictitious accounts given by Goldsmith himself; he seems to have visited Flanders, France, Germany, Switzerland, and Italy, living (as he was always to do) on the edge of destitution. He survived, to emerge in London in 1756, trying one job after another to subsist. Apothecary's assistant, unsuccessful (and unqualified) physician, possibly proof-reader, certainly an usher in a boy's school.

Gradually, however, he felt his way into the literary life. In 1757 he was writing articles on a regular basis for the *Monthly Review*, and earning a steady and reasonable income from it; by 1762 he had established himself as a writer worth respecting, with a wide set of friends in the literary world, including Samuel Johnson, whose career had run somewhat parallel to his. Although in 1760 he was earning the comfortable salary of £100 a year for writing two articles a week for John Newbery, these being the letters of a fictitious Chinaman reporting his amusing and penetratingly naïve impressions of England, he remained constantly in debt, his money draining away on gambling (which he was very bad at), elaborate and rather tasteless clothes, and other extravagances. In 1762 Newbery became his patron, landlord, and banker, and made him a strict allowance, to be debited against the credit earned by work done. This action explicitly acknowledged him to be the foremost journalistic talent in the stable of one of the most prominent publishers of the day, and worth the investment of a shrewd businessman. He took at this point another crucial step: he signed a contract for a *Survey of Experimental Philosophy*; that is, in order to make immediate money he was prepared to use the distinctive assurance and clarity of his prose style in producing compilations, translations, and other hack productions on matters of popular interest: a *History of England* (1764), a *Roman History* (1769), another *History of England* (1771), and the posthumously published *Grecian History* and *History of the Earth and Animated Nature* (1774). His life was to be bedevilled by debt, squandered advances, deadlines, and undone work; this is why, out of the voluminous quantity of his writings, relatively little is read now.

In 1764, however, he produced a major poem: *The Traveller, or a Prospect of Society*, a meditative account of his own wanderings in Europe. This piece was, remarkably, the first he had published under his own name, and it brought him fame, respect, and adulation. He was an eminent man; a founder-member, for instance, of what is still one of the most exclusive clubs in London: Dr Johnson's Club, whose membership has included most of the most eminent, witty, and talented people of their day. Reynolds (who became Goldsmith's closest friend), Sheridan, Gibbon, Burke, Fox, Garrick, Boswell, and so on for a long list.

In 1766 *The Vicar of Wakefield* was published. This wry, charming, and subtle tale, the *Book of Job* absurdly retold as comedy, whose sale had been used by Johnson to rescue the author from the bailiffs, was eventually to achieve an international fame, in spite of its author's lack of confidence in it and its hasty and patched-on ending; but not the kind of immediate pre-eminence and financial security that Goldsmith required.

The other route to such quick returns was through the theatre. Goldsmith's career as a playwright began with the first performance of *The Good Natured Man* early in 1768. The death of Newbery the previous December had made the need for wealth more pressing, but this rather feeble and ungainly comedy was a disappointingly moderate success.

In the last six years of his life he produced three important works of literature. The first was the nostalgic and rather sentimental pastoral *The Deserted Village* (1770); it is his most famous poem, but its value has slackened as the romanticism that brought it forth has ebbed and been replaced. The last was his *Retaliation*, written about two months before his death and posthumously published in 1774. To my mind it is his best poem: a satire on the set of literary friends to which he belonged, remarkable, like all of his best work, for its amalgam of kindness and telling, perceptive irony. And, thirdly, a year before he died, his best work and his only other play: the unique comedy, *She Stoops to Conquer*.

Goldsmith wrote the play in the summer of 1771, again under the pressure of debt, again attempting to catch at the golden and instantaneous rewards of a successful play. He had great difficulty in getting it staged, largely owing to the resistance of Colman and Garrick, the managers of London's two principal theatres. They thought that the play's overt attack on prevailing theatrical fashions made it too much of a risk. Garrick 'bought himself off by a poor prologue'[1] and Colman, eventually, reluctantly, put it on, at Covent Garden. The first night was at the tag-end of the season (15 March); leading actors had refused parts in it; the props and costumes were second-rate; and Colman had made no secret of his expectation that it would be damned. It was not. The first night audience was ecstatic, and audiences ever since have continued to laugh. The play has appeared in some *three hundred* different editions since 1773 and, since then, has been revived in the West End approximately once every three years, and almost constantly in provincial theatres.[2] It must be the most popular play outside Shakespeare.

Goldsmith, though temporarily exhilarated by its success, and the five hundred pounds that came with it, had no idea what he had created. He was soon submerged again in debt and depression, which did not leave him until his death in April 1774. This was tinged, like his life, with farce: his last act as a 'Doctor' was to poison himself, inadvertently, by persistent use of the wrong medicine. He left debts of £2,000.

SOURCES

Goldsmith's sources for *She Stoops to Conquer* were absurdly numerous. He was throughout his life an unscrupulous 'borrower' of other people's writings, and it is clear that his imagination needed the stimulus of raw material for re-working. For instance Marivaux's *Le Jeu de l'Amour et du Hasard* (1730), besides several explicit verbal parallels, has the heroine change places with her maid in order to assess her intended husband without him knowing it. Farquhar's *The Beaux' Stratagem* (1707) also has a number of

---

[1] Horace Walpole, *Letters*, ed. Peter Cunningham, V (Edinburgh, 1906), 453.
[2] Information from Susan Katherine Hamlyn, *She Stoops to Conquer: the Making of a Popular Success*, MA (unpublished), University of Birmingham, 1975. This thesis contains the best critical work on the play that I have yet seen.

textual similarities, and (among other, larger, parallels), the
wooing of the barmaid Cherry by the gentleman-in-disguise
Archer is strikingly similar. Ginger,[3] Goldsmith's latest and best
biographer, thinks (wrongly, I believe) that the play was based so
closely on Bickerstaffe's recent and successful opera *Love in a
Village* (1762) as to amount to evident and obvious plagiarism. And
so on; Hamlyn (*She Stoops to Conquer: the Making of a Popular
Success*, pp. 1–54) lists (*selectively*) over forty sources that have
been suggested for lines, scenes, incidents, characters, or the entire
structure. The proliferation of sources devalues the enterprise of
discovering them. None of these candidates comes very near
suggesting Goldsmith's unique play.

She Stoops to Conquer was, however, and in a rather different
way, dependent on other plays. It was written as an attack on an
important eighteenth-century theatrical movement: that known as
Sentimental Comedy. This aspect of the play is important, and has
never been treated in sufficient detail.

THE PLAY

She Stoops to Conquer is outstandingly a play that has survived and
cast off its context. It is extraordinarily *accessible*, and has been
popular for this (and other) reasons for 200 years. But the prologue, dedication, and epilogues proclaim that it was written as an
attack on a specific and allegedly predominant theatrical genre; and
its contemporary reception gives ample support for this view.
Moreover, the text of the play contains specific parodies of this
genre, and while these parodies remain marvellously and indepen-
dently absurd for the vast majority of readers and audiences who
have never read the minor comedy of the eighteenth century that is
under attack, it is worth re-locating this play in this context, if only
because such a comparison leads in to a more general consideration
of the play's structure and chief concerns.

The genre under attack is that of Sentimental Comedy. What
does this mean? From the play and its prologues and epilogues we
can gather what Goldsmith and Garrick thought it meant, at least:

1. It is *moral* comedy: it tends to rejoice in moral statements or 'sentiments' (Prologue, lines 25–30).
2. It is non-naturalistic ('Faces are blocks, in sentimental scenes') (Prologue, line 24).
3. It relies upon 'high-life scenes' and titled characters (Second
   Rejected Epilogue, ll. 33–6).
4. It is genteel comedy, without recourse to depicting 'low' characters
   or situations (I.ii, 35–45).

[3] John Ginger, *The Notable Man* (London, 1977).

Goldsmith's short 'Essay on the Theatre; or, a Comparison between Laughing and Sentimental Comedy'[4] which was published two months before *She Stoops to Conquer* and was clearly intended to prepare the way for that play, adds the following:

5. insipid dialogue
6. 'pathetic' scenes, in which we are invited to weep, rather than laugh.
7. 'good, and exceedingly generous' characters (p. 212).

Finally, we can add two more general characteristics that this list doesn't specify:

8. Sentimental Comedy is *benevolent*; its laughter is sympathetic rather than satiric, it depends on the notion that human nature is fundamentally good, or at least easily corrigible. Its villains are few, and the end of the play brings them (sometimes with alarming suddenness) to reform.
9. Finally, it is the comedy of *sensibility*; it rejoices in exhibiting in its characters a noble delicacy of sentiment, an emotional refinement often close to the modern pejorative use of 'sentimentality'.

This, then, is how people viewed the genre in 1773. It is easy to see these categories as a reaction against Restoration Comedy, conceived of as licentious, satiric, amoral, witty, often cruel, explicitly sexual, and, primarily, very *funny*. The problem, however, is that these categories do not hold as a simple binary opposition to characterize the plays of the 1760s and 1770s; on the one hand, Sentimental Comedy, on the other, Laughing Comedy, as exemplified by Goldsmith's play.[5] *She Stoops to Conquer*, for instance, simply does not embody solely a set of oppositions to these categories. Marlow, when he is reduced to inarticulacy by talking to Kate, produces a parody of moral 'sentiments' (1): for instance, 'The folly of most people is rather an object of mirth than uneasiness' (II.i, 418–19). But he is also capable of saying, as Kate is making the transition from barmaid to her own natural character,

> I can never harbour a thought of seducing simplicity that trusted in my honour, or bringing ruin upon one, whose only fault was being too lovely . . . I owe too much to the opinion of the world, too much to the authority of a father, so that—I can scarcely speak it—it affects me (IV.i, 226–9, 242–4)

---

[4] *Collected Works of Oliver Goldsmith*, ed. Arthur Friedman, III (Oxford, 1966), 209–13.

[5] This is the traditional view, as given in such standard works as Allardyce Nicoll's *History of English Drama, 1660–1900*, III (Cambridge, 1952), 124–54. But recent scholars, particularly Robert D. Hume in his 'Goldsmith and Sheridan and the Supposed Revolution of "Laughing" against "Sentimental" Comedy' (in *Studies in Change and Revolution*, ed. Paul J. Korshin [Menston, 1972]), have severely criticized the view, even going so far as to suggest that there was no such genre as Sentimental Comedy.

—thus giving voice to 'sentiments' (1), the pathetic (6), a rather mawkish goodness and generosity (7), a certain insipidity (5) and artificiality (2), 'benevolent' corrigibility (8), and, above all, sensibility (9). A number of the scenes with Hastings and Miss Neville, particularly their reform, apparently exhibit most of these characteristics. If we add to this the fact that Marlow's father is titled (3) and that most of the characters are genteel, and belong to the leisured gentry (4), we have (by a process of ruthlessly partial selection) found *all* of the 'Sentimental' characteristics in this 'Laughing' comedy.

What sense, then, can we make of the distinction? Firstly, there was indeed a loose genre called Sentimental Comedy, that gave birth to a number of plays throughout the eighteenth century, though not a predominant number, and which was characterized by some or most of the eight characteristics (except, curiously, the reliance on titled characters [6], which Goldsmith seems to have been deceived about). Its leading exponents were Cibber, Woodfall, and Kelly; no one but specialists now reads these plays. Goldsmith was reacting against *something*. Secondly, while the play evinces these characteristics to some extent, it also contains reactions against them; it operates, not only by parody, but by self-parody. It is as if Goldsmith sets up an opposition within the play between sentimentalism (as defined above) and its opposites: Restoration Comedy, satire, and farce. From the clash between the two he effects a synthesis, that we can identify as a comedy that both contains and transcends the limitations of these genres.

The farcical element has always hindered the appreciation and understanding of *She Stoops to Conquer*. Is its continued popularity solely because it is a very funny play, or is there more to it than that? Literary criticism, which is not designed to cope with humour, has largely ignored it,[6] thus assenting to the former view. This, too, was the reaction of the play's contemporary audience. 'The audience are kept in a continual roar' said the *Morning Chronicle*;[7] and Samuel Johnson said that he knew not of any 'comedy for many years, that has answered so much the great end of comedy—making an audience merry'.[8] But comedy is not solely defined by laughter; if this is all, then Horace Walpole's savage comments have some force: 'What play makes you laugh very much, and yet is a very wretched comedy? . . . the drift tends to no

[6] There are, of course, exceptions; for instance, Ginger and Hamlyn (op. cit.) have both written interestingly on the play, and there is an essay by B. Eugene McCarthy which is well worth reading (see *Further Reading*, p. xxix).

[7] 16 March 1773.

[8] James Boswell, *Life of Johnson*, ed. G. B. Hill, revised L. F. Powell, II (Oxford, 1934), 233.

moral, no edification of any kind'.[9] In other words, as the March issue of the *London Magazine* remarked, since 'consistency is repeatedly violated for the sake of humour . . in lieu of comedy he has sometimes presented us with farce'. And this, in general, is the view that has prevailed ever since: enshrined in the critics' silence and the audiences' laughter, the suspicion that the play is nothing but a highly successful farce.

I believe, and hope to show, that this is not so. It is easy to see why it came about. Goldsmith—and his audience—were reacting against self-consciously moral comedy, and the opposite of that is farce, which we can define as a mixture of ludicrous improbabilities and (as far as possible) a lack of moral concerns. The audience, and critics since, reacted too far, and identified the play with farce,[10] but Goldsmith did not.[11] The play does borrow from this genre, and continually flirts with it; its prime achievement as theatre is its energy, its pace; the action, and the laughter, never let up, and the play's timing in this respect is superb. It is the timing of good farce. But consider, for instance, the most nearly farcical moment in it, when Tony Lumpkin has persuaded his mother (soaked up to her waist in mud) to hide at the bottom of her own garden from her own husband as a highwayman. This, we may note, is the classic stratagem of farce, much of whose comic tension is in the tricks to get people out of the way so that the subterfuges are not brought to light. The urgent absurdity of the action hurries the audience past this in a gale of laughter, and thus it is easy to miss one crucial and rather poignant point: Mrs Hardcastle is the only unsympathetic character in the play—resolutely so, and irredeemably; she will not reform at the end. This is appropriately unsentimental; but nonetheless this absurd 'humours' character is given depth. She is prepared, with some heroism, to give up her life for her son. 'Take my life, my life, but spare that young gentleman, spare my child' (V.ii, 113–14), she screams, and the audience laughs at the farcical release of tension as the subterfuge is discovered; thus we miss her moment of grace. The most apparently farcical moment in the play also reveals a disturbing moral ambiguity: this over-poweringly selfish and vain woman has a completely selfless love for her 'graceless varlet' of a son. Goldsmith's joke is at the expense of those who cannot perceive it.

Another way in which the play contains Sentimentalism but expands beyond it is in its attitude to 'sentiments', the sententious sayings identified with Sentimental Comedy. As we have seen,

---

[9] op. cit., pp. 453, 467.   [10] For instance, Nicoll, op. cit., p. 159.
[11] That he believed that his play had a moral (but not moralizing) function can be seen in the second rejected epilogue, lines 14–30.

Marlow has a rather tedious tendency towards them; Hardcastle, too, is prone to strike attitudes: 'I could never teach the fools of this age, that the indigent world could be clothed out of the trimmings of the vain' (I.i, 92–4) and again 'modesty seldom resides in a breast that is not enriched with nobler virtues' (I.i, 134–5). But, as we have already seen with Mrs Hardcastle, it is important to the play's method to induce a double attitude towards its characters: neither the simplicities of farce nor the banalities of moralizing, but the reflexive subtleties of comedy. Hardcastle is a sympathetic character, as we see in the loving mutual mockery and mutual respect of his conversations with his daughter (e.g. I.i, 90–146), and his resigned affection for his appalling wife. But he is also absurdly pompous and complacent. He is punished for it by being roundly put down by Marlow, but the seeds of this comic retribution are already present in these two tendentious 'sentiments'. After all, it is his peculiar insistence on Kate wearing a plain dress that furthers the illusion that his house is an inn—to his discomfort (and, by another twist, to the play's happy resolution); and his remarking that modesty necessarily involves nobler virtues becomes a resounding dramatic irony at his expense when we consider what terrible things the undeniably modest Marlow is about to say and do to him.

Even Hastings and Miss Neville are, finally, subject to this ironic double perception. They are the weakest part of the play; they only seem to come alive as foils, Hastings to Marlow, Neville to Kate, and both (their main purpose) as pawns to be shoved enthusiastically around by Tony Lumpkin; Hastings's (sentimental) remark 'Perish the baubles! Your person is all I desire' (II.i, 345) is one of the very few unspeakable lines in the entire play. Their sub-plot is the essence of sentimental fiction, and so is their language. Miss Neville refuses to elope, for two reasons; one is realistic: 'My spirits are so sunk with the agitations I have suffered, that I am unable to face any new danger' (V.ii, 145–7). Considering that she has undergone precisely the same torments which Lumpkin has put his mother through—which Hastings, incidentally, seems to find rather funny (V.ii, 28)—this is understandable. However, the second reason is what the audience should be paying attention to: 'No, Mr Hastings; no. Prudence once more comes to my relief, and I will obey its dictates. In the moment of passion, fortune may be despised, but it ever produces a lasting repentance' (V.ii, 154–7). This curious mixture of moralizing and prudentiality is precisely the material of Sentimental Comedy, and the unpleasantly tactical humility is continued in their repentance speeches to the assembled elders. It is clear that Goldsmith is being (not uncharacteristically) careless about the peripheral details of his plot; one recalls his remark in his 'Comparison between Laughing and Sentimental Comedy', that the latter is 'of all others, the most easily written'.[12] However, the play, almost at the last minute, redeems itself, with an extraordinary wrench. Mrs Hardcastle's comment on this is 'Pshaw, pshaw, this is all but the whining end of a modern novel' (V.iii, 129–30). The play is avowedly against the sentimentality that Hastings and Neville represent; but the criticism, which specifically refers their behaviour to the literary genre, is put into the mouth of the play's only villain. Again, and this time with startling abruptness, the play turns on itself, its apparent simplicities becoming duplicity. It is, after all, a play about disguises; every important character in it at some point tells lies. The play also disguises itself, retreating behind these masks, leading us, as Marlow is led, by lies towards a recognition of our own complacencies.

The clearest instance of this mockery of the (London, sophisticated) audience is in the scene at the Three Jolly Pigeons. The audience, like the two gentlemen down from London, is introduced to the world of pastoral, in its role as mocking mirror of the securities of the metropolis, and both find it to be a world turned upside down. The play has begun with an opposition between town and country, between Hardcastle's attack on the vanity of the town and his wife's longing for its sophistication. But underneath this conventionality there is a dissonance. Marlow is unable to recognize that Tony Lumpkin is the Squire and thus of his own class, and from this his misfortunes (and salvation) arise. But the audience too is presented with an image of itself. Fashionable comedy was genteel; its audience was predominantly middle class; it damned that which did not correspond to its polite conception of itself with the penetrating shouted monosyllable '*low*'. By this means it had caused a scene from Goldsmith's first play to be removed from the stage. On the play's first night the London audience was presented with the sight of 'a low, paltry set of fellows' (I.i, 72) listening to the Squire's song, who suddenly, with marvellous inconsequentiality, start to pretend that they are a fashionable London audience: 'Oh damn anything that's *low*, I cannot bear it . . . the genteel thing is the genteel thing at any time' (I.ii, 38–9). This is in its own right very funny, and the audience of the time, like the modern audience that has lost the specific context, is once more swept past it by laughter. But it is not farce; it is very sharp satire. No wonder George Colman, the theatre's manager, felt during the first performance that he had been sitting on a powder-barrel.

---

[12] Friedman, op. cit., p. 213.

This particular opposition between 'genteel' and 'low', is a local and specific joke, another attack on what is now a dead genre, a dead audience, and their vanished complacencies; but (once more) it expands—this time through the entire play—into a perennial theme. The play is deeply concerned with the concept of social class, and examines it by a whole series of just such reversals. In this distorted pastoral world no one seems to know which class they belong to. The yokels claim with comic pomposity to be gentlemen: 'What though I am obligated to dance a bear, a man may be a gentleman for all that' (I.ii, 41–3) and Tony Lumpkin, with curious seriousness, asks them to go when Marlow and Hastings arrive: 'Gentlemen ... they mayn't be good enough company for you' (I.ii, 70–1). Tony himself is a kind of yokel, 'a poor contemptible booby' (IV.i, 390), but he is also a member of 'one of the best families in the county' (IV.i, 193–4) and Hardcastle seems to have more in common with his clumsy servants than with his genteel guests. The joke against him is rather sharp, as he later recognizes ('And yet he might have seen something in me above a common inn-keeper' [V.i, 15–16])—for the point is that without foreknowledge his guests *cannot* recognize him as intrinsically a gentleman; as Hastings remarks, with cruel superciliousness, he 'forgets that he's an inn-keeper, before he has learned to be a gentleman' (II.i, 200–2). And this redounds with equal sharpness on the two 'gentlemen'; is their rudeness to Hardcastle appropriate— 'gentlemanly'—behaviour towards *anyone*, whether landlord or landowner? Are *they* then intrinsically gentlemen? Hardcastle's mansion is indeed Liberty-Hall,[13] and the results are rather unnerving.

What Goldsmith wanted from comedy was that it should be 'perfectly satirical yet perfectly goodnatured'[14] at the same time. This apparently awkward blend of 'Sentimental' benevolence with 'Restoration' satire is precisely what he achieved in *She Stoops to Conquer*. The satire beneath the kindliness is felt but not perceived: the audience is too busy laughing.

The main way in which this is managed, apart from the kind of

---

[13] It is worth pointing out another specifically contemporary reference behind this theme. Goldsmith (a firm Tory) was writing this play while the movement for 'Wilkes and Liberty' was approaching its final flowering, and in a letter of 7 September 1771 that describes the composition of *She Stoops to Conquer*, he mentions, in passing, that 'the cry of Liberty is still as loud as ever' (quoted in Arthur Lytton Sells, *Oliver Goldsmith*, 1974, p. 146). Marlow's servant is a Wilkesian ('Though I'm but a servant, I'm as good as another man' [IV.i, 123]). The violently populist and libertarian Wilkes riots, which repeatedly convulsed London, add a curious resonance to the play's genial but ambiguous coinage, 'Liberty-Hall'.

[14] Goldsmith, *Monthly Review*, May 1773.

implicit undercutting I have tried to elucidate above, is in the curiously triadic structure of the play. There are three central characters, Lumpkin, Marlow, and Kate, and their relationship in the structure is triangular. Marlow is the manipulated focus of two plots, that of Lumpkin, which is satiric, and that of Kate, which is good-natured. Lumpkin's ruse brings out in him the Restoration rake, and Kate's the Sentimental lover. The final synthesis, the comic resolution, lies with Kate.

Let us start as the play does, with Tony Lumpkin, and with two critical comments. Kenrick, Goldsmith's enemy, was testily uncomprehending: 'The squire whom we are told to be a fool, proves the most sensible being of the piece'.[15] Not quite—there is Kate Hardcastle; but the paradox is well stated. A more modern critic is equally bemused, in fact awestruck:

> he has persistently reminded readers of such ideal creations of the comic imagination as Shakespeare's Puck. However exquisitely entertaining and flawlessly consistent, Goldsmith's booby is, one feels, not of earth. One wonders at him, as Shelley at the Skylark.[16]

Rather over-stated, but one knows what he means. The reference to Puck is apt. Tony Lumpkin, at once (like the play) laughed at and laughing at us, is, to begin with, the play's author. The plot is his creation; not only the subterfuge, but the liveliness and the timing are what he makes them, and the verbal energy is his language. Whenever the complicated twists of the plot (his plot) are about to founder, Lumpkin, like Puck, arrives, and whips and spurs it into action again, usually by heaping mistake upon mistake. His plot, his satire, the ambiguous Liberty-Hall, is suggested to him by the fact that the two Londoners cannot identify him as well-born, and so tell him exactly what they think of him; his revenge is that this honesty should be forced on them, to their discomfiture. Marlow tells Hardcastle just what he thinks of *him*. Thus Lumpkin embodies or creates all of the reversals (except Kate's) of 'genteel' and 'low' that the play contains, and his purpose is both farcical (he is a 'mere composition of tricks and mischief' [I.i, 39–40], a practical joker), and moral, an attribute in him that both Hardcastle (V.ii, 140) and Hastings (V.ii, 50) acknowledge. His paradox is therefore the play's: the moral farce. His energy is then deflected into the sub-plot (he is kept quite apart from his half-sister Kate, and never exchanges a word with her, as if even her integrity might be vulnerable to his wit), and into wickedly inventive tormenting of his mother. His character is completely untouched by the action of the play; benevolist notions of corrigi-

[15] *London Packet*, 24 March 1773.
[16] John Harrington Smith, 'Tony Lumpkin and the Country Booby Type in Antecedent English Comedy', *PMLA* LVIII (1943), 1049.

bility cannot contain him. When he gains his birthright, like Caliban, at the end, we feel obscurely that he has earned it; but unlike Caliban (whom he strongly resembles) he is unrepentant.

If Lumpkin is the play, Marlow suffers its action, and learns from it. The paradox of his character, the rake who is paralysed with shyness, can be seen quite easily in terms of literary genres (though of course it transcends these: he is curiously archetypal). He is at the beginning incapacitated from marriage, which is the golden resolution of comedy, by the fact that he is both too bold and too shy. He cannot love because he cannot talk of love; only either the false language of seduction, of besieging the ladies, of conquest, which is that of Restoration Comedy, or else the false platitudes of Sentimental Comedy. Symbolically, the latter make him dumb. His view of sex is that it can be bought: with noticeable explicitness for the 1770s it is made clear that he visits prostitutes and (ironically) will pay for the favours of the supposed barmaid. He relies on the securities of class-distinction, power, and money; he is, as Hardcastle points out, a bully (IV.i, 176) and thus his cowardice is a natural complement.

Described this way he seems very unpleasant; of course, and by a remarkable legerdemain, he is not. He is saved by his extreme vulnerability, by his comprehensive come-uppance, and by Kate. But it is worth noting that his redemption is not complete; he never quite gets his language right. He cannot stop being literary. His serious wooing is still, as we noticed, tinged with Sentiment, and though Kate rather likes it, she has its number beautifully: He 'said some civil things of my face, talked much of his want of merit, and the greatness of mine; mentioned his heart, gave a short tragedy speech, and ended with pretended rapture' (V.i, 106–9). And his last words as he stiffly unbends under her 'tormenting' are not fully redeemed: Kate is his possession, 'my little tyrant' (V.iii, 154). Nice, we may feel, that he is making an effort, but not quite right. The play's attack on the sentimentality of redemptions extends even here.

Finding a counterbalance to Tony Lumpkin for the second part of the play must have been difficult. It is remarkable that it didn't prove impossible. But Kate Hardcastle is equally Shakespearian in her origins; if Lumpkin is Puck, she reminds everyone of Rosalind in *As You Like It*. Like Lumpkin she is 'malicious' (III.i, 279), and (rather like Marlow) she has a frank appreciation of the financial aspects of what she is: 'a girl who brings her face to market' (III.i, 242).[17] Of course, she transcends this as well: her wit, resourceful-

[17] She was actually felt at the time to be rather shocking: 'the heroine has no more modesty than Lady Bridget', commented the sentimentally inclined Horace Walpole (op. cit., p. 453).

ness, and commonsense are constantly attractive. She is the only character actually and successfully in control of the Mistakes of the Night. She takes over Tony Lumpkin's satirical plot and makes it her own: an ameliorative, educational one. His comedy is destructive, mocking; hers heals, but is saved from sententiousness by her own mocking wit. She in fact appropriates all of the play's themes. She undergoes voluntarily (as no one else does) the reversal of class-roles, and does this in order to create a space for lovers to talk in that is independent of class and of the constrictions that reduce Marlow to lies or silence. She tells lies, but in order to force a truth; she turns near-farce into comedy; and she unites town and country in marriage. She is the prime agent of Goldsmith's synthesis of opposed genres. The play's happy ending is hers.

TEXTUAL NOTE

THE EARLIEST SURVIVING TEXT of *She Stoops to Conquer* is the manuscript (not in Goldsmith's handwriting) prepared before the first performance for the licenser for the theatre, now in the Larpent Collection of the Huntington Library, California (L). The first edition (73) appeared shortly after the play's run began, and sold so well (4,000 copies in three days) that it rapidly went through six impressions (73a–f). The first impression was carelessly printed, no doubt because of the rush caused by the play's unexpected success; it appears to have been set up in two different printing shops,[1] and thus has two different kinds of styling, one much more careless than the other. This situation was normalized in the second impression (73b) and it is on this that I have based my text; however, in accordance with New Mermaid practice the spelling of this edition is modernized, and the punctuation lightly normalized and clarified.

As to the words of *She Stoops to Conquer*, I have argued elsewhere[2] that the Larpent MS version records an alternative, and equally authoritative, version of the play, that survived in the theatre until well into the nineteenth century. This acting version is sometimes more vigorous and racy, and the more genteel printed readings may well have been imposed on the text against the will of the author. I have thus restored Larpent readings much more freely than is usual in modern editions and this edition prints many of them as part of the text for the first time since 1773.

The textual notes record all verbal emendations of 73b, plus the most significant rejected variants in L. The glosses annotate words that have become obscure. These are hardly noticed when the play is read, and particularly when it is watched, because of the marvellous vigour and clarity of its style; nonetheless, Goldsmith's urge towards naturalism and the 'low' caused him to locate the play firmly in the language habits of the 1770s. I have signalled this by giving the date of first usage of the glossed words as recorded in the *Oxford English Dictionary*. This shows a surprisingly large number

---

[1] See William B. Todd, 'The First Editions of *The Good-Natur'd Man* and *She Stoops to Conquer*', *Studies in Bibliography*, XI (1958), 133–42.

[2] Tom Davis and Susan Hamlyn, 'What do we do when two texts differ?', *Evidence in Literary Scholarship*, ed. René Wellek and Alvaro Ribeiro (Oxford, 1979), pp. 263–79.

TEXTUAL NOTE

of first usages and a reliance on words first used (in print) in the
eighteenth century. Not that Goldsmith was a word-coiner; but he
was often first or early in appropriating the spoken language of his
day into print. Glosses in quotation marks followed by '($S\mathcal{J}$)' are
from Johnson's *Dictionary* of 1755.

ABBREVIATIONS

ed.   editor
SJ   Samuel Johnson, *Dictionary*, 1755
s.d.   Stage direction
s.p.   Speech prefix
73a–f   The six impressions of the first edition of 1773
L   Larpent MS
om.   Omits
PMLA *Publications of the Modern Language Association of America*

FURTHER READING

Oliver Goldsmith, *Poems and Plays*, ed. Tom Davis (London, 1975).

Allardyce Nicoll, *A History of English Drama, 1660–1900*, III (Cambridge, 1952).

Goldsmith, the Critical Heritage, ed. G. S. Rousseau (London, 1974).

John Forster, *The Life and Adventures of Oliver Goldsmith* (London, 1848), revised 4th edition 1863.

Ricardo Quintana, *Oliver Goldsmith, a Georgian Study* (London, 1969).

Arthur Lytton Sells, *Les Sources françaises de Goldsmith* (Paris, 1924).

John Ginger, *The Notable Man* (London, 1977).

B. Eugene McCarthy, 'The Theme of Liberty in *She Stoops to Conquer*', *University of Windsor Review*, VII (1971), 1–8.

John Harrington Smith, 'Tony Lumpkin and the Country Booby Type in Antecedent English Comedy', *PMLA* LVIII (1943), 1038–49.

Robert D. Hume, 'Goldsmith and Sheridan and the Supposed Revolution of "Laughing" against "Sentimental" Comedy', *Studies in Change and Revolution*, ed. Paul J. Korshin (Menston, 1972), pp. 237–76.

She Stoops to Conquer:

O R,

The Mistakes of a Night.

A

C O M E D Y.

AS IT IS ACTED AT THE

T H E A T R E - R O Y A L

I N

C O V E N T - G A R D E N.

WRITTEN BY

Doctor G O L D S M I T H.

L O N D O N:

Printed for F. NEWBERY, in St. Paul's Church-Yard.

M DCC LXXIII.

TO SAMUEL JOHNSON, L.L.D.

Dear Sir,

By inscribing this slight performance to you, I do not mean so much to compliment you as myself. It may do me some honour to inform the public, that I have lived many years in intimacy with you. It may serve the interests of mankind also 5 to inform them, that the greatest wit may be found in a character, without impairing the most unaffected piety.

I have, particularly, reason to thank you for your partiality to this performance. The undertaking a comedy, not merely sentimental, was very dangerous; and Mr Colman, who saw 10 this piece in its various stages, always thought it so. However I ventured to trust it to the public; and though it was necessarily delayed till late in the season, I have every reason to be grateful.

I am Dear Sir, 15
Your most sincere friend,
And admirer,
OLIVER GOLDSMITH

---

10 *Colman* George Colman, the manager of Covent Garden, was extremely reluctant to put the play on because of its attack on the fashionable Sentimental Comedy (see Introduction). It was finally staged at the very end of the season.

PROLOGUE

By DAVID GARRICK, ESQ.

Enter MR WOODWARD,
Dressed in Black, and holding a Handkerchief to his Eyes

Excuse me, sirs, I pray—I can't yet speak—
I'm crying now—and have been all the week!
'Tis not alone this mourning suit, good masters;
I've that within——for which there are no plasters!
Pray would you know the reason why I'm crying?   5
The Comic muse, long sick, is now a-dying!
And if she goes, my tears will never stop;
For as a player, I can't squeeze out one drop:
I am undone, that's all—shall lose my bread—
I'd rather, but that's nothing—lose my head.   10
When the sweet maid is laid upon the bier,
Shuter and I shall be chief mourners here.
To *her* a mawkish drab of spurious breed,
Who deals in *sentimentals,* will succeed!
Poor *Ned* and *I* are dead to all intents,   15
We can as soon speak *Greek* as *sentiments!*
Both nervous grown, to keep our spirits up,
We now and then take down a hearty cup.
What shall we do?—If Comedy forsake us!
They'll turn us out, and no one else will take us;   20
But why can't I be moral?—Let me try—

---

1 s.d. WOODWARD Henry Woodward, a leading comic actor of his day, was
originally due to play Tony Lumpkin. He turned the part down, but agreed to
speak the prologue.
3–4 *'Tis not ... within* alluding to *Hamlet* I.ii, 77, 85, '"Tis not alone my inky cloak,
good mother ... But I have that within which passeth show'.
12 *Shuter* Ned Shuter, another leading comedian, played the part of Hardcastle.
14–16 *sentimentals ... sentiments* referring to the play's attack on Sentimental Comedy (see Introduction) with its characteristic pious moralizing, parodied in lines
25–30.
20 *They'll turn ... take us* quoting, for no apparent reason, Buckingham's *The
Rehearsal* (1671), II.iv, 'they'll turn us out, and nobody else will take us'.

My heart thus pressing—fixed my face and eye—
With a sententious look, that nothing means,
(Faces are blocks, in sentimental scenes)
Thus I begin—*All is not gold that glitters,*   25
Pleasure seems sweet, but proves a glass of bitters.
When ignorance enters, folly is at hand;
Learning is better far than house and land:
Let not your virtue trip, who trips may stumble,
And virtue is not virtue, if she tumble.   30
    I give it up—morals won't do for me;
To make you laugh I must play tragedy.
One hope remains—hearing the maid was ill,
A *doctor* comes this night to show his skill.
To cheer her heart, and give your muscles motion,   35
He in *five draughts* prepared, presents a potion:
A kind of magic charm—for be assured,
If you will *swallow it*, the maid is cured:
But desperate the Doctor, and her case is,
If you reject the dose, and make wry faces!   40
This truth he boasts, will boast it while he lives,
No *poisonous drugs* are mixed in what he gives;
Should he succeed, you'll give him his degree;
If not, within he will receive no fee!
The college *you*, must his pretensions back,   45
Pronounce him *regular*, or dub him *quack*.

---

24 *blocks* featureless wooden heads, used as wig-stands (1688)
30 *tumble* probably a sexual innuendo is implied
39 *Doctor* Goldsmith

---

46 *regular* properly qualified (1755). Perhaps a tactless allusion to the fact that 'Dr
   Goldsmith's' medical qualification was a product of his own imagination.

DRAMATIS PERSONAE

Men

SIR CHARLES MARLOW	*Mr Gardner*
YOUNG MARLOW (*his Son*)	*Mr Lewes*
HARDCASTLE	*Mr Shuter*
HASTINGS	*Mr Dubellamy*
TONY LUMPKIN	*Mr Quick*
DIGGORY	*Mr Saunders*

Women

MRS HARDCASTLE	*Mrs Green*
MISS HARDCASTLE	*Mrs Bulkely*
MISS NEVILLE	*Mrs Kniveton*
MAID	*Miss Willems*

LANDLORD, SERVANTS, *&c. &c.*

SHE STOOPS TO CONQUER:

or,

THE MISTAKES OF A NIGHT

Act I, Scene i

Scene. A Chamber in an old fashioned House

Enter MRS HARDCASTLE *and* MR HARDCASTLE

MRS HARDCASTLE

I vow, Mr Hardcastle, you're very particular. Is there a
creature in the whole country, but ourselves, that does not
take a trip to town now and then, to rub off the rust a little?
There's the two Miss Hoggs, and our neighbour, Mrs
Grigsby, go to take a month's polishing every winter. 5

HARDCASTLE

Ay, and bring back vanity and affectation to last them the
whole year. I wonder why London cannot keep its own
fools at home? In my time, the follies of the town crept
slowly among us, but now they travel faster than a stage-
coach. Its fopperies come down, not only as inside passen- 10
gers, but in the very basket.

MRS HARDCASTLE

Ay, *your* times were fine times, indeed; you have been
telling us of *them* for many a long year. Here we live in an
old rumbling mansion, that looks for all the world like an
inn, but that we never see company. Our best visitors are 15
old Mrs Oddfish, the curate's wife, and little Cripplegate,
the lame dancing-master: and all our entertainment your

2 *country* 'the place which any man inhabits, or in which he at present resides' (*SJ*;
1297)
11 *basket* the outside back seat or baggage-container of a stagecoach (first usage)
14 *rumbling* rambling. Apparently, perhaps ironically, an old-fashioned usage by
1773

She Stoops to Conquer 73 (The Novel L) L preserves the play's original title,
which was (like much about this play) changed at the last moment.
16 *Cripplegate* The names of the minor characters in this play usually mean something: here '-gate' means 'gait', or way of walking.

old stories of Prince Eugene and the Duke of Marlborough. I hate such old-fashioned trumpery.

HARDCASTLE

And I love it. I love everything that's old: old friends, old   20
times, old manners, old books, old wine; and I believe,
Dorothy, (*Taking her hand*) you'll own I have been pretty
fond of an old wife.

MRS HARDCASTLE

Lord, Mr Hardcastle, you're for ever at your 'Dorothys'
and your 'old wifes'. You may be a Darby, but I'll be no   25
Joan, I promise you. I'm not so old as you'd make me, by
more than one good year. Add twenty to twenty, and make
money of that.

HARDCASTLE

Let me see; twenty added to twenty, makes just fifty and
seven.   30

MRS HARDCASTLE

It's false, Mr Hardcastle: I was but twenty when I was
brought to bed of Tony, that I had by Mr Lumpkin, my
first husband; and he's not come to years of discretion yet.

HARDCASTLE

Nor ever will, I dare answer for him. Ay, you have taught
him finely.   35

MRS HARDCASTLE

No matter, Tony Lumpkin has a good fortune. My son is
not to live by his learning. I don't think a boy wants much
learning to spend fifteen hundred a year.

HARDCASTLE

Learning, quotha! A mere composition of tricks and mischief.   40

MRS HARDCASTLE

Humour, my dear: nothing but humour. Come, Mr Hardcastle, you must allow the boy a little humour.

HARDCASTLE

I'd sooner allow him an horse-pond. If burning the foot-
men's shoes, frighting the maids, and worrying the kittens,

19 *trumpery* 'something of no value; trifles' (*SJ*; 1531)
25–6 *Darby … Joan* an ageing affectionate couple (1735)
41 *Humour … humour* 73 (spirit … spirit L)

18–19 *Prince … Marlborough* respectively leaders of the Austrian and British
     armies against the French in the War of the Spanish Succession (1701–14).
43 *horse-pond* a pond for watering and washing horses. Hardcastle intends the
     proverbial meaning, as a place for ducking nuisances.

be humour, he has it. It was but yesterday he fastened my 45
wig to the back of my chair, and when I went to make a
bow, I popped my bald head in Mrs Frizzle's face.

MRS HARDCASTLE

And am I to blame? The poor boy was always too sickly to
do any good. A school would be his death. When he comes
to be a little stronger, who knows what a year or two's Latin 50
may do for him?

HARDCASTLE

Latin for him! A cat and fiddle. No, no, the ale-house and
the stable are the only schools he'll ever go to.

MRS HARDCASTLE

Well, we must not snub the poor boy now, for I believe we
shan't have him long among us. Anybody that looks in his 55
face may see he's consumptive.

HARDCASTLE

Ay, if growing too fat be one of the symptoms.

MRS HARDCASTLE

He coughs sometimes.

HARDCASTLE

Yes, when his liquor goes the wrong way.

MRS HARDCASTLE

I'm actually afraid of his lungs. 60

HARDCASTLE

And truly so am I; for he sometimes whoops like a speaking
trumpet—(TONY *hallooing behind the Scenes*)—Oh there he
goes—A very consumptive figure, truly.

Enter TONY, *crossing the Stage*

MRS HARDCASTLE

Tony, where are you going, my charmer? Won't you give
papa and I a little of your company, lovey? 65

TONY

I'm in haste, mother, I cannot stay.

MRS HARDCASTLE

You shan't venture out this raw evening, my dear: you look
most shockingly.

---

52 *cat and fiddle* proverbial: an unlikely combination
54 *snub* 'to check; to reprimand' (*SJ*; 1340)
61–2 *speaking trumpet* megaphone. Presumably Tony whoops as if he is shouting
  through one

TONY

I can't stay, I tell you. The Three Pigeons expects me
down every moment. There's some fun going forward.   70

HARDCASTLE

Ay; the ale-house, the old place: I thought so.

MRS HARDCASTLE

A low, paltry set of fellows.

TONY

Not so low neither. There's Dick Muggins the exciseman,
Jack Slang the horse doctor, Little Aminadab that grinds
the music box, and Tom Twist that spins the pewter   75
platter.

MRS HARDCASTLE

Pray, my dear, disappoint them for one night at least.

TONY

As for disappointing *them*, I should not so much mind; but
I can't abide to disappoint *myself*.

MRS HARDCASTLE (*Detaining him*)

You shan't go.   80

TONY

I will, I tell you.

MRS HARDCASTLE

I say you shan't.

TONY

We'll see which is strongest, you or I.

Exit, hauling her out

HARDCASTLE

Ay, there goes a pair that only spoil each other. But is not
the whole age in a combination to drive sense and discre-   85
tion out of doors? There's my pretty darling Kate; the
fashions of the times have almost infected her too. By
living a year or two in town, she is come to be fond of
gauze, and French frippery, as the best of them.

Enter MISS HARDCASTLE

75–6 *pewter platter* cf. 'another sung to a plate which he kept trundling on the edges'
(Goldsmith, *Works*, ed. Friedman, III [1966], 9)
88 *is come to be* L (is 73)
89 *gauze* 73 (gauze and Paris nets L)

73–4 *Dick Muggins ... Aminadab* A muggins is a fool (first usage); 'slang' meant
'humbug, nonsense' (1762); and Aminadab was a Jew, in the Bible the father-
in-law of Aaron (see e.g. Luke 3:33). Their names reveal them to be extremely
'low'.

HARDCASTLE
    Blessings on my pretty innocence! Dressed out as usual,   90
    my Kate. Goodness! What a quantity of superfluous silk
    hast thou got about thee, girl! I could never teach the fools
    of this age, that the indigent world could be clothed out of
    the trimmings of the vain.
MISS HARDCASTLE
    You know our agreement, sir. You allow me the morning   95
    to receive and pay visits, and to dress in my own manner;
    and in the evening, I put on my housewife's dress to please
    you.
HARDCASTLE
    Well, remember I insist on the terms of our agreement;
    and, by the bye, I believe I shall have occasion to try your   100
    obedience this very evening.
MISS HARDCASTLE
    I protest, sir, I don't comprehend your meaning.
HARDCASTLE
    Then, to be plain with you, Kate, I expect the young
    gentleman I have chosen to be your husband from town
    this very day. I have his father's letter, in which he informs   105
    me his son is set out, and that he intends to follow himself
    shortly after.
MISS HARDCASTLE
    Indeed! I wish I had known something of this before. Bless
    me, how shall I behave? It's a thousand to one I shan't like
    him; our meeting will be so formal, and so like a thing of   110
    business, that I shall find no room for friendship or
    esteem.
HARDCASTLE
    Depend upon it, child, I'll never control your choice; but
    Mr Marlow, whom I have pitched upon, is the son of my
    old friend, Sir Charles Marlow, of whom you have heard   115
    me talk so often. The young gentleman has been bred a
    scholar, and is designed for an employment in the service
    of his country. I am told he's a man of an excellent under-
    standing.
MISS HARDCASTLE
    Is he?   120
HARDCASTLE
    Very generous.

92 *hast* L (has 73)
114 *pitched* decided (1628)

MISS HARDCASTLE
I believe I shall like him
HARDCASTLE
Young and brave.
MISS HARDCASTLE
I'm sure I shall like him.
HARDCASTLE
And very handsome.   125
MISS HARDCASTLE
My dear papa, say no more (*Kissing his hand*), he's mine,
I'll have him.
HARDCASTLE
And to crown all, Kate, he's one of the most bashful and
reserved young fellows in all the world.
MISS HARDCASTLE
Eh! you have frozen me to death again. That word   130
reserved, has undone all the rest of his accomplishments. A
reserved lover, it is said, always makes a suspicious hus-
band.
HARDCASTLE
On the contrary, modesty seldom resides in a breast that is
not enriched with nobler virtues. It was the very feature in   135
his character that first struck me.
MISS HARDCASTLE
He must have more striking features to catch me, I promise
you. However, if he be so young, so handsome, and so
everything you mention, I believe he'll do still. I think I'll
have him.   140
HARDCASTLE
Ay, Kate, but there is still an obstacle. It's more than an
even wager, he may not have *you*.
MISS HARDCASTLE
My dear papa, why will you mortify one so?—Well, if he
refuses, instead of breaking my heart at his indifference,
I'll only break my glass for its flattery, set my cap to some   145
newer fashion, and look out for some less difficult admirer.
HARDCASTLE
Bravely resolved! In the meantime I'll go prepare the
servants for his reception; as we seldom see company they
want as much training as a company of recruits, the first
day's muster.   *Exit* 150

139 *everything* L (everything, as 73)
150 *muster* military inspection (1400)

MISS HARDCASTLE

Lud, this news of papa's puts me all in a flutter. Young, handsome; these he put last; but I put them foremost. Sensible, good-natured; I like all that. But then reserved, and sheepish, that's much against him. Yet can't he be cured of his timidity, by being taught to be proud of his 155 wife? Yes, and can't I—But I vow I'm disposing of the husband, before I have secured the lover.

Enter MISS NEVILLE

MISS HARDCASTLE

I'm glad you're come, Neville, my dear. Tell me, Constance, how do I look this evening? Is there anything whimsical about me? Is it one of my well-looking days, 160 child? Am I in face today?

MISS NEVILLE

Perfectly, my dear. Yet now I look again—bless me!—sure no accident has happened among the canary birds or the gold fishes? Has your brother or the cat been meddling? Or has the last novel been too moving? 165

MISS HARDCASTLE

No; nothing of all this. I have been threatened—I can scarce get it out—I have been threatened with a lover.

MISS NEVILLE

And his name——

MISS HARDCASTLE

Is Marlow.

MISS NEVILLE

Indeed! 170

MISS HARDCASTLE

The son of Sir Charles Marlow.

MISS NEVILLE

As I live, the most intimate friend of Mr Hastings, *my* admirer. They are never asunder. I believe you must have seen him when we lived in town.

MISS HARDCASTLE

Never. 175

MISS NEVILLE

He's a very singular character, I assure you. Among

160 *whimsical* odd, unusual (1675)

163–5 *accident . . . moving* mocking the appropriate 'sentimental' response to Kate's news of her intended lover, which is compared (with irony on both their parts) to the death of a pet or the experience of reading a fashionably mawkish novel.

women of reputation and virtue, he is the modestest man
alive; but his acquaintance give him a very different
character among creatures of another stamp: you under-
stand me.   180

MISS HARDCASTLE

An odd character, indeed. I shall never be able to manage
him. What shall I do? Pshaw, think no more of him, but
trust to occurrences for success. But how goes on your own
affair my dear, has my mother been courting you for my
brother Tony, as usual?   185

MISS NEVILLE

I have just come from one of our agreeable tête-à-têtes. She
has been saying a hundred tender things, and setting off
her pretty monster as the very pink of perfection.

MISS HARDCASTLE

And her partiality is such, that she actually thinks him so.
A fortune like yours is no small temptation. Besides, as she   190
has the sole management of it, I'm not surprised to see her
unwilling to let it go out of the family.

MISS NEVILLE

A fortune like mine, which chiefly consists in jewels, is no
such mighty temptation. But at any rate if my dear Hastings be but constant, I make no doubt to be too hard for her   195
at last. However, I let her suppose that I am in love with
her son, and she never once dreams that my affections are
fixed upon another.

MISS HARDCASTLE

My good brother holds out stoutly. I could almost love him
for hating you so.   200

MISS NEVILLE

It is a good-natured creature at bottom, and I'm sure
would wish to see me married to anybody but himself. But
my aunt's bell rings for our afternoon's walk round the
improvements. *Allons*. Courage is necessary as our affairs
are critical.   205

MISS HARDCASTLE

Would it were bedtime and all were well.   *Exeunt*

---

187 *setting off* praising, giving a flattering description of (1625)
194 *mighty temptation* 73 (great catch L)
204 *improvements* refer to the current fashion for landscape gardening

---

188 *pink of perfection* the first use of this phrase.
206 *Would ... well* cf. *1 Henry IV*, V.i,126: 'I would 'twere bed-time, Hal, and all
were well'.

Act I, Scene ii

*Scene. An Alehouse Room. Several shabby fellows, with Punch
and Tobacco.* TONY *at the head of the Table, a little higher than
the rest: a mallet in his hand.*

ALL

Hurrah, hurrah, hurrah, bravo.

FIRST FELLOW

Now, gentlemen, silence for a song. The Squire is going to
knock himself down for a song.

ALL

Ay, a song, a song.

TONY

Then I'll sing you, gentlemen, a song I made upon this   5
ale-house, the Three Pigeons.

SONG

Let school-masters puzzle their brain,
    With grammar, and nonsense, and learning;
Good liquor, I stoutly maintain,
    Gives genus a better discerning.   10
Let them brag of their Heathenish Gods,
    Their Lethes, their Styxes, and Stygians;
Their Quis, and their Quæs, and their Quods,
    They're all but a parcel of Pigeons.
            Toroddle, toroddle, toroll.   15

When Methodist preachers come down,
    A preaching that drinking is sinful,
I'll wager the rascals a crown,
    They always preach best with a skinful.

10 *genus* dialect pronunciation of 'genius': a Lumpkinism
12 *Lethe . . . Styx* rivers of the classical underworld; from the latter came the
    adjective 'Stygian'
13 *Quis . . . Quods* the nominative forms of the Latin relative pronoun, learned by
    rote by every schoolboy, for whom a knowledge of the language and mythology
    of Rome was made practically synonymous with 'learning'
14 *Pigeons* fools, dupes (1593)
16 *Methodist preachers* the itinerant open-air preachers who followed a network of
    circuits all over Britain, preaching Wesleyan revivalism, and teetotalism

---

3 *knock . . . song* nominate himself for a song, with a tap of the 'mallet in his hand'
    (s.d.). But probably an unkind pun on the auctioneering use of 'knock down':
    sell himself for nothing, show himself to be worthless.

But when you come down with your pence,   20
   For a slice of their scurvy religion,
I'll leave it to all men of sense,
   But you my good friend are the pigeon.
        Toroddle, toroddle, toroll.

Then come, put the jorum about,   25
   And let us be merry and clever,
Our hearts and our liquors are stout,
   Here's the Three Jolly Pigeons for ever.
Let some cry up woodcock or hare,
   Your bustards, your ducks, and your widgeons;   30
But of all the birds in the air,
   Here's a health to the Three Jolly Pigeons.
        Toroddle, toroddle, toroll.

ALL
Bravo, bravo.
FIRST FELLOW
The Squire has got spunk in him.   35
SECOND FELLOW
I love to hear him sing, bekeays he never gives us nothing
that's *low*.
THIRD FELLOW
Oh damn anything that's *low*, I cannot bear it.
FOURTH FELLOW
The genteel thing is the genteel thing at any time. If so be
that a gentleman bees in a concatenation accordingly.   40
THIRD FELLOW
I like the maxum of it, Master Muggins. What though I am
obligated to dance a bear, a man may be a gentleman for all
that. May this be my poison if my Bogie shall ever dance

---

25 *jorum* bowl of punch (1730)
35 *spunk* spirit, natural ardour (first usage)
41 *maxum* i.e. maxim: moral precept, sententious saying (1594); the yokels are
being 'Sentimental'
43 *Bogie . . . dance* L (bear ever dances 73)

---

40 *concatenation* 'an uninterrupted unvariable succession' (*SJ*; 1622). Meaningless
here. The yokels are pretending to be of the same class as the Squire, unsuccess-
fully; at the same time Goldsmith is mocking the bourgeois niceties of his
audience, who had condemned his last play as 'low'.

but to the very genteelest of tunes. 'Water parted', or the
minuet in *Ariadne*.   45

SECOND FELLOW

What a pity it is the Squire is not come to his own. It would
be well for all the publicans within ten miles round of him.

TONY

Ecod and so it would Master Slang. I'd then show what it
was to keep choice of company.

SECOND FELLOW

Oh he takes after his own father for that. To be sure old   50
Squire Lumpkin was the finest gentleman I ever set my
eyes on. For winding the straight horn, or beating a thicket
for a hare, or a wench, he never had his fellow. It was a
saying in the place, that he kept the best horses, dogs, and
girls in the whole county.   55

TONY

Ecod, and when I'm of age I'll be no bastard I promise you.
I have been thinking of Bet Bouncer and the miller's grey
mare to begin with. But come, my boys, drink about and
be merry, for you pay no reckoning. Well Stingo, what's
the matter?   60

Enter LANDLORD

LANDLORD

There be two gentlemen in a post-chaise at the door. They
have lost their way upo' the forest; and they are talking
something about Mr Hardcastle.

TONY

As sure as can be one of them must be the gentleman that's
coming down to court my sister. Do they seem to be   65
Londoners?

LANDLORD

I believe they may. They look woundily like Frenchmen.

TONY

Then desire them to step this way, and I'll set them right in
a twinkling.   *Exit* LANDLORD

44 *Water parted* an aria from Thomas Augustine Arne's opera *Artaxerxes* (1762)
45 *Ariadne* Handel's opera *Arianna in Creta* (1734). The famous minuet forms part
   of the overture
56 *bastard* 73 (Changeling L)
59 *Stingo* was a slang word for strong ale or beer (1635)
61 *post-chaise* a closed travelling-carriage for up to four people, with the driver
   sitting on one of the horses; a succession of hired horses was used, from stage to
   stage (1712)
67 *woundily* extremely (1706)

Gentlemen, as they mayn't be good enough company for   70
you, step down for a moment, and I'll be with you in the
squeezing of a lemon.   *Exeunt Mob*

TONY
Father-in-law has been calling me whelp, and hound, this
half-year. Now if I pleased, I could be so revenged upon
the old grumbletonian. But then I'm afraid—afraid of   75
what! I shall soon be worth fifteen hundred a year, and let
him frighten me out of *that* if he can.

Enter LANDLORD, *conducting* MARLOW *and* HASTINGS

MARLOW
What a tedious uncomfortable day have we had of it! We
were told it was but forty miles across the country, and we
have come above threescore.   80

HASTINGS
And all, Marlow, from that unaccountable reserve of
yours, that would not let us enquire more frequently on the
way.

MARLOW
I own, Hastings, I am unwilling to lay myself under an
obligation to everyone I meet; and often stand the chance   85
of an unmannerly answer.

HASTINGS
At present, however, we are not likely to receive any
answer.

TONY
No offence, gentlemen. But I'm told you have been enquir-
ing for one Mr Hardcastle, in these parts. Do you know   90
what part of the country you are in?

HASTINGS
Not in the least, sir, but should thank you for information.

TONY
Nor the way you came?

HASTINGS
No, sir; but if you can inform us——

TONY
Why, gentlemen, if you know neither the road you are   95
going, nor where you are, nor the road you came, the first
thing I have to inform you is, that—You have lost your
way.

73 *Father-in-law* step-father (1552)
75 *grumbletonian* grumbler (first usage)
90 *these* L (those 73)

MARLOW

We wanted no ghost to tell us that.

TONY

Pray, gentlemen, may I be so bold as to ask the place from   100
whence you came?

MARLOW

That's not necessary towards directing us where we are to
go.

TONY

No offence; but question for question is all fair, you know.
Pray, gentlemen, is not this same Hardcastle a cross-   105
grained, old-fashioned, whimsical fellow, with an ugly
face, a daughter, and a pretty son?

HASTINGS

We have not seen the gentleman, but he has the family you
mention.

TONY

The daughter, a tall trapesing, trolloping, talkative   110
maypole—The son, a pretty, well-bred, agreeable youth,
that everybody is so fond of.

MARLOW

Our information differs in this. The daughter is said to be
well-bred and beautiful; the son, an awkward booby, re-
ared up and spoiled at his mother's apron-string.   115

TONY

He-he-hem!—Then, gentlemen, all I have to tell you is,
that you won't reach Mr Hardcastle's house this night, I
believe.

HASTINGS

Unfortunate!

TONY

It's a damned long, dark, boggy, dirty, dangerous way.   120
Stingo, tell the gentlemen the way to Mr Hardcastle's;
(*Winking upon the* LANDLORD) Mr Hardcastle's, of Quag-
mire Marsh, you understand me.

LANDLORD

Master Hardcastle's! Lock-a-daisy, my masters, you're
come a deadly deal wrong! When you came to the bottom   125
of the hill, you should have crossed down Squash Lane.

112 *so fond* L (fond 73)
126 *Squash Lane* 'squash' meant 'splash', so presumably a boggy track is implied

99 *ghost* another fashionable allusion to Shakespeare: 'There needs no ghost, my
lord, come from the grave/To tell us this' (*Hamlet*, I.v, 125–26).

MARLOW (*Noting it down*)
Cross down Squash Lane!

LANDLORD
Then you were to keep straight forward, till you came to
four roads.

MARLOW *(Still noting)*
Come to where four roads meet!   130

TONY
Ay; but you must be sure to take only one of them.

MARLOW
O sir, you're facetious.

TONY
Then keeping to the right, you are to go sideways till you
come upon Crack-skull Common: there you must look
sharp for the track of the wheel, and go forward, till you   135
come to farmer Murrain's barn. Coming to the farmer's
barn, you are to turn to the right, and then to the left, and
then to the right about again, till you find out the old
mill—

MARLOW (*Who had been noting*)
Zounds, man! we could as soon find out the longitude!   140

HASTINGS
What's to be done, Marlow?

MARLOW
This house promises but a poor reception; though perhaps
the Landlord can accommodate us.

LANDLORD
Alack, master, we have but one spare bed in the whole
house.   145

TONY
And to my knowledge, that's taken up by three lodgers
already. (*After a pause, in which the rest seem disconcerted*) I
have hit it. Don't you think, Stingo, our landlady could

---

127 s.d. *Noting it down* L (om. 73)
130 s.d. *Still noting* L (om. 73)
140 s.d. *Who had been noting* L (om. 73)

134–6 *Crack-skull Common … Murrain's* The countryside is made to sound uninvit-
ingly Gothic and dangerous. Unmetalled rural lanes had deep ruts (the 'track of
the wheel') which could break a horse's leg, hence 'Crack-skull common'; a
murrain was a plague (1330).
140 *longitude* a prize of £20,000 had been on offer since 1713 for a precise means of
discovering the longitude. It was won, in fact, three months after this play
opened.

accommodate the gentlemen by the fire-side, with—three
chairs and a bolster? 150

HASTINGS

I hate sleeping by the fire-side.

MARLOW

And I detest your three chairs and a bolster.

TONY

You do, do you?—then let me see—what if you go on a
mile further, to the Buck's Head; the old Buck's Head on
the hill, one of the best inns in the whole county? 155

HASTINGS

O ho! so we have escaped an adventure for this night,
however.

LANDLORD (*Apart to* TONY)

Sure, you ben't sending them to your father's as an inn, be
you?

TONY

Mum, you fool you. Let *them* find that out. (*To them*) You 160
have only to keep on straight forward, till you come to a
large old house by the roadside. You'll see a pair of large
horns over the door. That's the sign. Drive up the yard,
and call stoutly about you.

HASTINGS

Sir, we are obliged to you. The servants can't miss the 165
way?

TONY

No, no: But I must tell you though, the landlord is rich,
and going to leave off business; so he wants to be thought a
gentleman, saving your presence, he! he! he! He'll be for
giving you his company, and ecod if you mind him, he'll 170
persuade you that his mother was an alderman, and his
aunt a Justice of Peace.

LANDLORD

A troublesome old blade to be sure; but a' keeps as good
wines and beds as any in the whole country.

MARLOW

Well, if he supplies us with these, we shall want no further 175
connection. We are to turn to the right, did you say?

167 *must tell* L (tell 73)
176 *connection* (personal) relationship (1768)

TONY

No, no; straight forward. I'll just step myself, and show you a piece of the way. (*To the* LANDLORD) Mum.

LANDLORD

Ah, bless your heart, for a sweet, pleasant——damned mischievous son of a whore.   *Exeunt*   180

Act II, Scene i

Scene. An old-fashioned House

Enter HARDCASTLE, *followed by three or four awkward*
SERVANTS

HARDCASTLE
Well, I hope you're perfect in the table exercise I have been
teaching you these three days. You all know your posts and
your places, and can show that you have been used to good
company, without ever stirring from home.
SERVANTS
Ay, ay.   5
HARDCASTLE
When company comes, you are not to pop out and stare,
and then run in again, like frighted rabbits in a warren.
SERVANTS
No, no.
HARDCASTLE
You, Diggory, whom I have taken from the barn, are to
make a show at the side-table; and you, Roger, whom I   10
have advanced from the plough, are to place yourself be-
hind *my* chair. But you're not to stand so, with your hands
in your pockets. Take your hands from your pockets,
Roger; and from your head, you blockhead you. See how
Diggory carries his hands. They're a little too stiff, indeed,   15
but that's no great matter.
DIGGORY
Ay, mind how I hold them. I learned to hold my hands this
way, when I was upon drill for the militia. And so being
upon drill——
HARDCASTLE
You must not be so talkative, Diggory. You must be all   20
attention to the guests. You must hear us talk, and not
think of talking; you must see us drink, and not think of
drinking; you must see us eat, and not think of eating.
DIGGORY
By the laws, your worship, that's perfectly unpossible.
When ever Diggory sees yeating going forward, ecod he's   25
always wishing for a mouthful himself.

---

18 *militia* the organized citizens' army of non-professional soldiers, that acted as a
'home' or 'national' guard

HARDCASTLE

Blockhead! Is not a belly-full in the kitchen as good as a
belly-full in the parlour? Stay your stomach with that
reflection.

DIGGORY

Ecod I thank your worship, I'll make a shift to stay my   30
stomach with a slice of cold beef in the pantry.

HARDCASTLE

Diggory, you are too talkative. Then if I happen to say a
good thing, or tell a good story at table, you must not all
burst out a-laughing, as if you made part of the company.

DIGGORY

Then ecod your worship must not tell the story of Ould   35
Grouse in the gun-room: I can't help laughing at that—he!
he! he!—for the soul of me. We have laughed at that these
twenty years—ha! ha! ha!

HARDCASTLE

Ha! ha! ha! The story is a good one. Well, honest Diggory,
you may laugh at that—but still remember to be attentive.   40
Suppose one of the company should call for a glass of wine,
how will you behave? A glass of wine, sir, if you
please—(*To* DIGGORY) Eh, why don't you move?

DIGGORY

Ecod, your worship, I never have courage till I see the
eatables and drinkables brought upo' the table, and then   45
I'm as bauld as a lion.

HARDCASTLE

What, will nobody move?

FIRST SERVANT

I'm not to leave this pleace.

SECOND SERVANT

I'm sure it's no pleace of mine.

THIRD SERVANT

Nor mine, for sartain.   50

DIGGORY

Wauns, and I'm sure it canna be mine.

HARDCASTLE

You numbskulls! and so while, like your betters, you are
quarrelling for places, the guests must be starved. Oh you
dunces! I find I must begin all over again.——But don't I

---

36 *Grouse* a common name for a dog; no connotation yet of 'grumble'

51 *Wauns* wounds, short for 'god's wounds' (1694)

53 *places* a pun: 'place' could mean simply 'position', as now, or 'government
appointment' (1558)

hear a coach drive into the yard? To your posts, you   55
blockheads. I'll go in the meantime and give my old
friend's son a hearty reception at the gate.

Exit HARDCASTLE

DIGGORY

By the elevens, my pleace is gone quite out of my head.

ROGER

I know that my pleace is to be everywhere.

FIRST SERVANT

Where the devil is mine?   60

SECOND SERVANT

My pleace is to be nowhere at all; and so Ize go about my
business.

Exeunt SERVANTS, *running about as if frighted, different ways*

Enter SERVANT *with Candles, showing in* MARLOW *and*
HASTINGS

SERVANT

Welcome, gentlemen, very welcome. This way.

HASTINGS

After the disappointments of the day, welcome once more,
Charles, to the comforts of a clean room and a good fire.   65
Upon my word, a very well-looking house; antique, but
creditable.

MARLOW

The usual fate of a large mansion. Having first ruined the
master by good housekeeping, it at last comes to levy
contributions as an inn.   70

HASTINGS

As you say, we passengers are to be taxed to pay all these
fineries. I have often seen a good sideboard, or a marble
chimneypiece, though not actually put in the bill, inflame a
reckoning confoundedly.

MARLOW

Travellers, George, must pay in all places. The only   75
difference is, that in good inns, you pay dearly for luxuries;
in bad ones, you are fleeced and starved.

HASTINGS

You have lived pretty much among them. In truth, I have
been often surprised, that you who have seen so much of

58 *By the elevens* obscure; only found in Goldsmith. 'Heavens'? 'Apostles' (minus
    Judas)?
69 *good housekeeping* hospitality (1538)
77 *ones* L (inns 73)

the world, with your natural good sense, and your many   80
opportunities, could never yet acquire a requisite share of
assurance.

MARLOW

The Englishman's malady. But tell me, George, where
could I have learned that assurance you talk of? My life has
been chiefly spent in a college, or an inn, in seclusion from   85
that lovely part of the creation that chiefly teach men
confidence. I don't know that I was ever familiarly
acquainted with a single modest woman—except my
mother—But among females of another class you know—

HASTINGS

Ay, among them you are impudent enough of all consci-   90
ence.

MARLOW

They are of *us* you know.

HASTINGS

But in the company of women of reputation I never saw
such an idiot, such a trembler; you look for all the world as
if you wanted an opportunity of stealing out of the room.   95

MARLOW

Why man that's because I *do* want to steal out of the room.
Faith, I have often formed a resolution to break the ice,
and rattle away at any rate. But I don't know how, a single
glance from a pair of fine eyes has totally overset my
resolution. An impudent fellow may counterfeit modesty,   100
but I'll be hanged if a modest man can ever counterfeit
impudence.

HASTINGS

If you could but say half the fine things to them that I have
heard you lavish upon the barmaid of an inn, or even a
college bedmaker—   105

MARLOW

Why, George, I can't say fine things to them. They freeze,
they petrify me. They may talk of a comet, or a burning
mountain, or some such bagatelle. But to me, a modest
woman, dressed out in all her finery, is the most tremen-
dous object of the whole creation.   110

HASTINGS

Ha! ha! ha! At this rate, man, how can you ever expect to
marry!

MARLOW

Never, unless as among kings and princes, my bride were
to be courted by proxy. If, indeed, like an Eastern bride-
groom, one were to be introduced to a wife he never saw   115

before, it might be endured. But to go through all the
terrors of a formal courtship, together with the episode of
aunts, grandmothers, and cousins, and at last to blurt out
the broad staring question, of, 'Madam, will you marry
me?' No, no, that's a strain much above me I assure you.   120

HASTINGS

I pity you. But how do you intend behaving to the lady you
are come down to visit at the request of your father?

MARLOW

As I behave to all other ladies. Bow very low. Answer yes,
or no, to all her demands—But for the rest, I don't think I
shall venture to look in her face, till I see my father's again.   125

HASTINGS

I'm surprised that one who is so warm a friend can be so
cool a lover.

MARLOW

To be explicit, my dear Hastings, my chief inducement
down was to be instrumental in forwarding your happiness, not my own. Miss Neville loves you, the family don't   130
know you, as my friend you are sure of a reception, and let
honour do the rest.

HASTINGS

My dear Marlow! But I'll suppress the emotion. Were I a
wretch, meanly seeking to carry off a fortune, you should
be the last man in the world I would apply to for assistance.   135
But Miss Neville's person is all I ask, and that is mine, both
from her deceased father's consent, and her own inclination.

MARLOW

Happy man! You have talents and art to captivate any
woman. I'm doomed to adore the sex, and yet to converse   140
with the only part of it I despise. This stammer in my
address, and this awkward professing visage of mine, can
never permit me to soar above the reach of a milliner's
'prentice, or one of the duchesses of Drury Lane. Pshaw!
this fellow here to interrupt us.   145

117 *terrors* 73 (terms L)
119 *staring* glaringly conspicuous (1513)
142 *professing* L (prepossessing 73). 'Professing' in the sense of 'to make a show of
    any sentiments by loud declaration' (*SJ*; 1601); i.e. Marlow is prone to
    blushing
144 *duchesses of Drury Lane* 'duchess' was a slang term for a woman of showy
    appearance (1700); here it means either an actress at the Theatre Royal,
    Drury Lane, or, more likely, one of the prostitutes who worked outside for the
    benefit of the playgoers

Enter HARDCASTLE

HARDCASTLE

Gentlemen, once more you are heartily welcome. Which is
Mr Marlow? Sir, you're heartily welcome. It's not my way,
you see, to receive my friends with my back to the fire. I
like to give them a hearty reception in the old style at my
gate. I like to see their horses and trunks taken care of.   150

MARLOW *(Aside)*

He has got our names from the servants already. *(To him)*
We approve your caution and hospitality, sir. *(To* HAST-
INGS*)* I have been thinking, George, of changing our
travelling dresses in the morning. I am grown confoundedly ashamed of mine.   155

HARDCASTLE

I beg, Mr Marlow, you'll use no ceremony in this house.

HASTINGS

I fancy, Charles, you're right: the first blow is half the
battle. I intend opening the campaign with the white and
gold.

HARDCASTLE

Mr Marlow—Mr Hastings—gentlemen—pray be under   160
no constraint in this house. This is Liberty-Hall, gentlemen. You may do just as you please here.

MARLOW

Yet, George, if we open the campaign too fiercely at first,
we may want ammunition before it is over. I think to
reserve the embroidery to secure a retreat.   165

HARDCASTLE

Your talking of a retreat, Mr Marlow, puts me in mind of
the Duke of Marlborough, when we went to besiege
Denain. He first summoned the garrison.

MARLOW

Don't you think the *ventre d'or* waistcoat will do with the
plain brown?   170

HARDCASTLE

He first summoned the garrison, which might consist of
about five thousand men——

157 *Charles* L (George 73)   161 *Liberty-Hall* Goldsmith's own coinage
165 *retreat* 73 (following this L has an extra speech: Hast. And the Spring velvet
   brings up mine)   169 *Ventre d'or* gold-fronted, presumably

158–9 *campaign . . . white and gold* i.e. begin to lay siege to the ladies, with the aid of a
   coat and waistcoat of (probably) different colours, a fashion just beginning and
   therefore particularly smart in the 1770s.

HASTINGS

I think not: brown and yellow mix but very poorly.

HARDCASTLE

I say, gentlemen, as I was telling you, he summoned the garrison, which might consist of about five thousand 175 men——

MARLOW

The girls like finery.

HARDCASTLE

Which might consist of about five thousand men, well appointed with stores, ammunition, and other implements of war. Now, says the Duke of Marlborough, to George 180 Brooks, that stood next to him—You must have heard of George Brooks; I'll pawn my Dukedom, says he, but I take that garrison without spilling a drop of blood. So——

MARLOW

What, my good friend, if you gave us a glass of punch in the meantime, it would help us to carry on the siege with 185 vigour.

HARDCASTLE

Punch, sir! (*Aside*) This is the most unaccountable kind of modesty I ever met with.

MARLOW

Yes, sir, punch. A glass of warm punch, after our journey, will be comfortable. This is Liberty-Hall, you know. 190

HARDCASTLE

Here's Cup, sir.

MARLOW (*Aside*)

So this fellow, in his Liberty-Hall, will only let us have just what he pleases.

191 *Cup* sweetened and spiced wine (first usage)

180–2 *The Duke of Marlborough ... George Brooks*. Hardcastle cannot have been at Denain; nor was Marlborough, nor George Brooks, whom Hardcastle expects Marlow to have heard of (he is 'my friend Bruce' in the L version of III.i, 52–3), since this person seems never to have existed. Marlborough was recalled to England before the (unsuccessful) siege, which was conducted by the Dutch (eleven thousand, not five), the British troops under Ormonde having been withdrawn. Moreover, it is difficult to understand how Marlborough could both 'summon the garrison' (i.e. the *defenders* of an invested town [1542]) and offer to 'take that garrison' (i.e. overcome the defenders). Finally, these events took place in 1712, some sixty years before the presumably contemporary action of the play. Clearly Hardcastle is not only lying, but talking complete nonsense, about the campaign; moreover, he is also, like his wife, lying about his age. Goldsmith, incidentally, was well aware of what happened at Denain (see his *History of England*, iv [1771], 166, 178).

HARDCASTLE (*Taking the Cup*)

I hope you'll find it to your mind. I have prepared it with
my own hands, and I believe you'll own the ingredients are   195
tolerable. Will you be so good as to pledge me, sir? Here,
Mr Marlow, here is to our better acquaintance.   *Drinks*

MARLOW (*Aside*)

A very impudent fellow this! but he's a character, and I'll
humour him a little. Sir, my service to you.   *Drinks*

HASTINGS (*Aside*)

I see this fellow wants to give us his company, and forgets   200
that he's an inn-keeper, before he has learned to be a
gentleman.

MARLOW

From the excellence of your Cup, my old friend, I suppose
you have a good deal of business in this part of the country.
Warm work, now and then, at elections, I suppose.   205

HARDCASTLE

No, sir, I have long given that work over. Since our betters
have hit upon the expedient of electing each other, there's
no business for us that sell ale.

HASTINGS

So, then you have no turn for politics I find.

HARDCASTLE

Not in the least. There was a time, indeed, I fretted myself   210
about the mistakes of government, like other people; but
finding myself every day grow more angry, and the
government growing no better, I left it to mend itself.
Since that, I no more trouble my head about Hyder Ali, or
Ali Cawn, than about Ally Croaker. Sir, my service to you.   215

205 *Warm work ... elections* i.e. in bribing voters with free drink
206–8 *Since ... ale* 73 (L has this crossed out with two large X's; perhaps a
censorship)

206–7 *our betters ... each other* probably refers to electoral corruption by the large
landowners who more or less controlled the vote in the small constituencies that
they owned outright. Thus there would be no point in working for the election
of a rival candidate.
208 *for us that sell ale*. Hardcastle himself is probably alluding rather awkwardly to
the proverbial expression 'thus it must be, if we sell ale'—i.e. if we undertake
sordid or lucrative employment. See Swift's *A Complete Collection of Genteel
and Ingenious Conversation* (1738), p. 466.
214–15 *Hyder Ali ... Croaker* Hyder Ali was a maharaja of Mysore. Ali Cawn
(Khan) was either the subah of Bengal who was known for his cruelty and
corruption, or his son-in-law, who deposed him in 1761. Ally Croker was a
character in a popular Irish song, a line from which is quoted in George
Colman's *The Jealous Wife* (1761): 'Will you marry me, dear Ally, Ally Croker?'

HASTINGS

So what with eating above stairs, and drinking below, with
receiving your friends without, and amusing them within,
you lead a good pleasant bustling life of it.

HARDCASTLE

I do stir about a great deal, that's certain. Half the
differences of the parish are adjusted in this very parlour.   220

MARLOW (*After drinking*)

And you have an argument in your Cup, old gentleman,
better than any in Westminster-Hall.

HARDCASTLE

Ay, young gentleman, that, and a little philosophy.

MARLOW (*Aside*)

Well, this is the first time I ever heard of an inn-keeper's
philosophy.   225

HASTINGS

So then, like an experienced general, you attack them on
every quarter. If you find their reason manageable, you
attack it with your philosophy; if you find they have no
reason, you attack them with this. Here's your health, my
philosopher.   *Drinks* 230

HARDCASTLE

Good, very good, thank you; ha! ha! Your Generalship
puts me in mind of Prince Eugene, when he fought the
Turks at the battle of Belgrade. You shall hear.

MARLOW

Instead of the battle of Belgrade, I believe it's almost time
to talk about supper. What has your philosophy got in the   235
house for supper?

HARDCASTLE

For supper, sir! (*Aside*) Was ever such a request to a man in
his own house!

MARLOW

Yes, sir, supper sir; I begin to feel an appetite. I shall make
devilish work tonight in the larder, I promise you.   240

HARDCASTLE (*Aside*)

Such a brazen dog sure never my eyes beheld. (*To him*)
Why really, sir, as for supper I can't well tell. My Dorothy,
and the cook-maid, settle these things between them. I
leave these kind of things entirely to them.

216 *what* L (that 73)
217 *without ... within* L (within ... without 73)
222 *Westminster-Hall* where the law-courts were situated
233 *Belgrade* the siege (not battle) of Belgrade took place in 1717

MARLOW

You do, do you?   245

HARDCASTLE

Entirely. By the bye, I believe they are in actual consulta-
tion upon what's for supper this moment in the kitchen.

MARLOW

Then I beg they'll admit *me* as one of their privy council.
It's a way I have got. When I travel, I always choose to
regulate my own supper. Let the cook be called. No   250
offence I hope, sir.

HARDCASTLE

O no, sir, none in the least; yet I don't know how: our
Bridget, the cook-maid, is not very communicative upon
these occasions. Should we send for her, she might scold us
all out of the house.   255

HASTINGS

Let's see your list of the larder then. I ask it as a favour. I
always match my appetite to my bill of fare.

MARLOW (*To* HARDCASTLE, *who looks at them with surprise*)

Sir, he's very right, and it's my way too.

HARDCASTLE

Sir, you have a right to command here. Here, Roger, bring
us the bill of fare for tonight's supper. I believe it's drawn   260
out. Your manner, Mr Hastings, puts me in mind of my
uncle, Colonel Wallop. It was a saying of his, that no man
was sure of his supper till he had eaten it.

Enter ROGER, *who gives a Bill of Fare*

HASTINGS (*Aside*)

All upon the high ropes! His uncle a Colonel! We shall
soon hear of his mother being a Justice of Peace. But let's   265
hear the bill of fare.

MARLOW (*Perusing*)

What's here? For the first course; for the second course;
for the dessert. The devil, sir, do you think we have

263 s.d. *Enter ... Fare* L (om. 73)
264 *All upon the high ropes* on his high horse (1700)

260 *supper* Supper was served at 10 p.m. or later, and was not the main meal of the
day, which would have been eaten at 3 or 4. It usually consisted of cold meats.
The point of the ensuing confusion is that the meal Hardcastle offers was not
unusually elaborate for the occasion, but was much more formal and sumptu-
ous than might be expected at an inn.

brought down the whole Joiners Company, or the
Corporation of Bedford, to eat up such a supper? Two or   270
three little things, clean and comfortable, will do.

HASTINGS

But, let's hear it.

MARLOW (*Reading*)

For the first course at the top, a pig's face, and prune sauce.

HASTINGS

Damn your pig's face, I say.

MARLOW

And damn your prune sauce, say I.   275

HARDCASTLE

And yet, gentlemen, to men that are hungry, a pig's face,
with prune sauce, is very good eating.

MARLOW

At the bottom, a calf's tongue and brains.

HASTINGS

Let your brains be knocked out, my good sir; I don't like
them.   280

MARLOW

Or you may clap them on a plate by themselves. I do.

HARDCASTLE (*Aside*)

Their impudence confounds me. (*To them*) Gentlemen,
you are my guests, make what alterations you please. Is
there anything else you wish to retrench or alter, gentlemen?   285

MARLOW

Item. A pork pie, a boiled rabbit and sausages, a florentine, a shaking pudding, and a dish of tiff—tuff—taffety
cream!

269–70 *Joiners Company ... Corporation of Bedford* The ancient trade guilds ('companies') and city councils ('Corporations') were known for their banquets

273, 278 *at the top ... At the bottom* it was usual in a formal menu to specify the
positioning of the dishes on the table

273–6 *pig's face ... pig's face ... pig's face* L (pig ... pig ... a pig 73)

286–7 *florentine* a pie or tart, especially a meat pie, usually but not always containing
spinach (1567)

287 *shaking pudding* eggs, cream, and a little flour boiled for an hour with flavour-
ings; i.e. a blancmange (not in *OED*)

287–8 *taffety cream* a dish of fine silky cream (i.e. with the consistency of taffeta)
using finely ground spices and fine sugar (first usage)

HASTINGS

Confound your made dishes, I shall be as much at a loss in
this house as at a green and yellow dinner at the French 290
ambassador's table. I'm for plain eating.

HARDCASTLE

I'm sorry, gentlemen, that I have nothing you like, but if
there be anything you have a particular fancy to——

MARLOW

Why, really, sir, your bill of fare is so exquisite, that any
one part of it is full as good as another. Send us what you 295
please. So much for supper. And now to see that our beds
are aired, and properly taken care of.

HARDCASTLE

I entreat you'll leave all that to me. You shall not stir a step.

MARLOW

Leave that to you! I protest, sir, you must excuse me, I
always look to these things myself. 300

HARDCASTLE

I must insist, sir, you'll make yourself easy on that head.

MARLOW

You see I'm resolved on it. (*Aside*) A very troublesome
fellow this, as ever I met with.

HARDCASTLE

Well, sir, I'm resolved at least to attend you. (*Aside*) This
may be modern modesty, but I never saw anything look so 305
like old-fashioned impudence.

Exeunt MARLOW *and* HARDCASTLE

HASTINGS

So I find this fellow's civilities begin to grow troublesome.
But who can be angry at those assiduities which are meant
to please him? Ha! what do I see? Miss Neville, by all that's
happy! 310

Enter MISS NEVILLE

MISS NEVILLE

My dear Hastings! To what unexpected good fortune? to
what accident am I to ascribe this happy meeting?

HASTINGS

Rather let me ask the same question, as I could never have
hoped to meet my dearest Constance at an inn.

289 *made dish* a dish made up of several ingredients (1621). 'Made dishes are
esteemed by the politest companies' (Charlotte Cartwright, *The Lady's Best
Companion* [1789], p. 26)
290 *green ... dinner* referring to the colour of the elaborate sauces, perhaps

MISS NEVILLE

An inn! sure you mistake! my aunt, my guardian, lives   315
here. What could induce you to think this house an inn?

HASTINGS

My friend Mr Marlow, with whom I came down, and I,
have been sent here as to an inn, I assure you. A young
fellow whom we accidentally met at a house hard by
directed us hither.   320

MISS NEVILLE

Certainly it must be one of my hopeful cousin's tricks, of
whom you have heard me talk so often, ha! ha! ha! ha!

HASTINGS

He whom your aunt intends for you? He of whom I have
such just apprehensions?

MISS NEVILLE

You have nothing to fear from him, I assure you. You'd   325
adore him if you knew how heartily he despises me. My
aunt knows it too, and has undertaken to court me for him,
and actually begins to think she has made a conquest.

HASTINGS

Thou dear dissembler! You must know, my Constance, I
have just seized this happy opportunity of my friend's visit   330
here to get admittance into the family. The horses that
carried us down are now fatigued with their journey, but
they'll soon be refreshed; and then if my dearest girl will
trust in her faithful Hastings, we shall soon be landed in
France, where even among slaves the laws of marriage are   335
respected.

MISS NEVILLE

I have often told you, that though ready to obey you, I yet
should leave my little fortune behind with reluctance. The
greatest part of it was left me by my uncle, the India
Director, and chiefly consists in jewels. I have been for   340
some time persuading my aunt to let me wear them. I fancy
I'm very near succeeding. The instant they are put into my
possession you shall find me ready to make them and
myself yours.

HASTINGS

Perish the baubles! Your person is all I desire. In the   345

---

335   *the laws of marriage* Because the two brothers of George III had made private
marriages, an unpopular Royal Marriage Act was passed in 1772, restricting
relations of the King from marrying at will. William Henry, Duke of Glouces-
ter, one of the offending brothers, was present at the first night of this play, and
the audience, taking this line as an attack on the Act, applauded it violently.

meantime, my friend Marlow must not be let into his
mistake. I know the strange reserve of his temper is such,
that if abruptly informed of it, he would instantly quit the
house before our plan was ripe for execution.

MISS NEVILLE

But how shall we keep him in the deception? Miss Hard-   350
castle is just returned from walking; what if we still continue to deceive him?——This, this way—— *They confer*

Enter MARLOW

MARLOW

The assiduities of these good people tease me beyond
bearing. My host seems to think it ill manners to leave me
alone, and so he claps not only himself but his old-   355
fashioned wife on my back. They talk of coming to sup
with us too; and then, I suppose, we are to run the gauntlet
through all the rest of the family.—What have we got
here!—

HASTINGS

My dear Charles! Let me congratulate you!—The most   360
fortunate accident!—Who do you think is just alighted?

MARLOW

Cannot guess.

HASTINGS

Our mistresses my boy, Miss Hardcastle and Miss Neville.
Give me leave to introduce Miss Constance Neville to your
acquaintance. Happening to dine in the neighbourhood,   365
they called on their return to take fresh horses here. Miss
Hardcastle has just stepped into the next room, and will be
back in an instant. Wasn't it lucky? eh?

MARLOW (*Aside*)

I have just been mortified enough of all conscience, and
here comes something to complete my embarrassment.   370

HASTINGS

Well! but wasn't it the most fortunate thing in the world?

MARLOW

Oh! yes. Very fortunate—a most joyful encounter——
But our dresses, George, you know, are in disorder——What if we should postpone the happiness till
tomorrow?——Tomorrow at her own house——It will be   375
every bit as convenient—And rather more respectful——Tomorrow let it be.   *Offering to go*

363 *my boy* L (boy 73)

MISS NEVILLE

By no means, sir. Your ceremony will displease her. The disorder of your dress will show the ardour of your impatience. Besides, she knows you are in the house, and will 380 permit you to see her.

MARLOW

Oh! the devil! how shall I support it? Hem! hem! Hastings, you must not go. You are to assist me, you know. I shall be confoundedly ridiculous.

HASTINGS

Pshaw man! it's but the first plunge, and all's over. She's 385 but a woman, you know.

MARLOW

And of all women, she that I dread most to encounter! Yet, hang it! I'll take courage. Hem!

Enter MISS HARDCASTLE *as returned from walking, with a Bonnet on, &c.*

HASTINGS (*Introducing them*)

Miss Hardcastle, Mr Marlow, I'm proud of bringing two persons of such merit together, that only want to know, to 390 esteem each other.

MISS HARDCASTLE (*Aside*)

Now for meeting my modest gentleman with a demure face, and quite in his own manner. (*After a pause, in which he appears very uneasy and disconcerted*) I'm glad of your safe arrival, sir——I'm told you had some accidents by the 395 way.

MARLOW

Only a few madam. Yet we had some. Yes, madam, a good many accidents, but should be sorry—madam—or rather glad of any accidents—that are so agreeably concluded. Hem! 400

HASTINGS (*To him*)

You never spoke better in your whole life. Keep it up, and I'll ensure you the victory.

MISS HARDCASTLE

I'm afraid you flatter, sir. You that have seen so much of the finest company can find little entertainment in an obscure corner of the country. 405

387–8 *Yet . . . Hem!* ed. (1773 assigns this to the end of Marlow's previous speech. L omits it altogether)

388 s.d. *with a Bonnet on* L (a Bonnet 73) 397 *Yet* L (Yes, 73)

MARLOW (*Gathering courage*)

I have lived, indeed, in the world, madam; but I have kept
very little company. I have been but an observer upon life,
madam, while others were enjoying it.

MISS NEVILLE

But that, I am told, is the way to enjoy it at last.

HASTINGS (*To him*)

Cicero never spoke better. Once more, and you are con-   410
firmed in assurance for ever.

MARLOW (*To him*)

Hem! Stand by me then, and when I'm down, throw in a
word or two to set me up again.

MISS HARDCASTLE

An observer, like you, upon life, were, I fear, disagreeably
employed, since you must have had much more to censure   415
than to approve.

MARLOW

Pardon me, madam. I was always willing to be amused.
The folly of most people is rather an object of mirth than
uneasiness.

HASTINGS (*To him*)

Bravo, Bravo. Never spoke so well in your whole life. Well!   420
Miss Hardcastle, I see that you and Mr Marlow are going
to be very good company. I believe our being here will but
embarrass the interview.

MARLOW

Not in the least, Mr Hastings. We like your company of all
things. (*To him*) Zounds! George, sure you won't go? How   425
can you leave us?

HASTINGS

Our presence will but spoil conversation, so we'll retire to
the next room. (*To him*) You don't consider, man, that we
are to manage a little tête-à-tête of our own.

Exeunt HASTINGS *and* MISS NEVILLE

MISS HARDCASTLE (*After a pause*)

But you have not been wholly an observer, I presume, sir: 430
the ladies I should hope have employed some part of your
addresses.

MARLOW (*Relapsing into timidity*)

Pardon me, madam, I—I—I—

MISS HARDCASTLE

Then why take such pains to study and observe them?

433–5 *I—I—I . . . deserve them* (I—I—I as yet have studied—only—to—deserve
them 73)

MARLOW

As yet I have studied—only—to—deserve them.   435

MISS HARDCASTLE

And that some say is the very worst way to obtain them.

MARLOW

Perhaps so, madam. But I love to converse only with the more grave and sensible part of the sex.——But I'm afraid I grow tiresome.

MISS HARDCASTLE

Not at all, sir; there is nothing I like so much as grave   440
conversation myself; I could hear it for ever. Indeed I have often been surprised how a man of sentiment could ever admire those light airy pleasures, where nothing reaches the heart.

MARLOW

It's——a disease——of the mind, madam. In the variety   445
of tastes there must be some who wanting a relish——for——um-a-um.

MISS HARDCASTLE

I understand you, sir. There must be some, who wanting a relish for refined pleasures, pretend to despise what they are incapable of tasting.   450

MARLOW

My meaning, madam, but infinitely better expressed. And I can't help observing——a——

MISS HARDCASTLE (*Aside*)

Who could ever suppose this fellow impudent upon some occasions? (*To him*) You were going to observe, sir——

MARLOW

I was observing, madam——I protest, madam, I forget   455
what I was going to observe.

MISS HARDCASTLE (*Aside*)

I vow and so do I. (*To him*) You were observing, sir, that in this age of hypocrisy—something about hypocrisy, sir.

MARLOW

Yes, madam. In this age of hypocrisy there are few who upon strict enquiry do not—a—a—a——   460

MISS HARDCASTLE

I understand you perfectly, sir.

MARLOW (*Aside*)

Egad! and that's more than I do myself.

---

436 *some say* 73 (same way L)
438 *sensible* having sensibility; capable of delicate emotion (1675)

MISS HARDCASTLE

You mean that in this hypocritical age there are few that do
not condemn in public what they practise in private, and
think they pay every debt to virtue when they praise it.   465

MARLOW

True, madam; those who have most virtue in their
mouths, have least of it in their bosoms. But I'm sure I tire
you, madam.

MISS HARDCASTLE

Not in the least, sir; there's something so agreeable and
spirited in your manner, such life and force—pray, sir, go   470
on.

MARLOW

Yes, madam. I was saying——that there are some
occasions——when a total want of courage, madam, des-
troys all the——and puts us——upon a——a——a——

MISS HARDCASTLE

I agree with you entirely, a want of courage upon some   475
occasions assumes the appearance of ignorance, and be-
trays us when we most want to excel. I beg you'll proceed.

MARLOW

Yes, madam. Morally speaking, madam—but I see Miss
Neville expecting us in the next room. I would not intrude
for the world.   480

MISS HARDCASTLE

I protest, sir, I never was more agreeably entertained in all
my life. Pray go on.

MARLOW

Yes, madam. I was——But she beckons us to join her.
Madam, shall I do myself the honour to attend you?

MISS HARDCASTLE

Well then, I'll follow.   485

MARLOW (*Aside*)

This pretty smooth dialogue has done for me.   *Exit*

MISS HARDCASTLE

Ha! ha! ha! Was there ever such a sober sentimental interview? I'm certain he scarce looked in my face the whole
time. Yet the fellow, but for his unaccountable bashful-
ness, is pretty well too. He has good sense, but then so   490
buried in his fears, that it fatigues one more than ignorance. If I could teach him a little confidence, it would be
doing somebody that I know of a piece of service. But who
is that somebody?—that, faith, is a question I can scarce
answer.   *Exit*   495

Enter TONY *and* MISS NEVILLE, *followed by* MRS HARDCASTLE
and HASTINGS

TONY

What do you follow me for, cousin Con? I wonder you're
not ashamed to be so very engaging.

MISS NEVILLE

I hope, cousin, one may speak to one's own relations, and
not be to blame.

TONY

Ay, but I know what sort of a relation you want to make me   500
though; but it won't do. I tell you, cousin Con, it won't do,
so I beg you'll keep your distance, I want no nearer relationship.

She follows coqueting him to the Back Scene

MRS HARDCASTLE

Well! I vow, Mr Hastings, you are very entertaining.
There's nothing in the world I love to talk of so much as   505
London, and the fashions, though I was never there
myself.

HASTINGS

Never there! You amaze me! From your air and manner, I
concluded you had been bred all your life either at
Ranelagh, St James's, or Tower Wharf.   510

MRS HARDCASTLE

Oh! Sir, you're only pleased to say so. We country persons
can have no manner at all. I'm in love with the town, and
that serves to raise me above some of our neighbouring
rustics; but who can have a manner, that has never seen the

---

514 *manner* a fashionable air (1694)

503 s.d. *Back Scene* The eighteenth-century stage consisted of a proscenium stage
that projected into the audience, where the main action took place, and an open
box behind it, with wings or 'side scenes' projecting into it. The back was
formed by two shutters that met in the middle, called the 'back scenes'. All of
the scenes ran in grooves, and could be moved in and out by invisible scene-
shifters, who could interchange them with other scenes for a 'change of scene'.
Entrances were made through two stage doors which were in front of the
side-scenes and behind the proscenium stage.

510 *Ranelagh ... Tower Wharf.* Hastings is mocking her provincial ignorance: St
James's and Ranelagh were fashionable centres, whereas Tower Wharf was
distinctly not.

Pantheon, the Grotto Gardens, the Borough, and such   515
places where the Nobility chiefly resort? All I can do, is to
enjoy London at second-hand. I take care to know every
tête-à-tête from the *Scandalous Magazine*, and have all the
fashions, as they come out, in a letter from the two Miss
Rickets of Crooked Lane. Pray how do you like this head,   520
Mr Hastings?

HASTINGS

Extremely elegant and *dégagée*, upon my word, madam.
Your *Friseur* is a Frenchman, I suppose?

MRS HARDCASTLE

I protest I dressed it myself from a print in the *Ladies
Memorandum-book* for the last year.   525

HASTINGS

Indeed. Such a head in a side-box, at the Playhouse, would
draw as many gazers as my Lady Mayoress at a City Ball.

MRS HARDCASTLE

I vow, since inoculation began, there is no such thing to be
seen as a plain woman; so one must dress a little particular
or one may escape in the crowd.   530

HASTINGS

But that can never be your case, madam, in any dress.

Bowing

MRS HARDCASTLE

Yet, what signifies *my* dressing when I have such a piece of

---

520 *head* her hair has been elaborately built up over a stuffed frame (1494)
522 *dégagée* relaxed, informal; the opposite of Mrs Hardcastle's hairstyle
523 *Friseur* hairdresser (1750)
528 *inoculation* against smallpox, a general practice by 1722 (half a century before,
   that is)

515–16 *Pantheon . . . resort.* Only the Pantheon (in Oxford Street) was a resort of the
   nobility; the Grotto Gardens was a cheap version of Ranelagh, and the
   Borough (of Southwark), once the address of the nobility, was by 1773 largely
   inhabited by rich tradesmen.
518 *tête-à-tête . . . Scandalous Magazine.* Each number of the *Town and Country
   Magazine* contained an engraved head of a famous man and his mistress, with a
   scandalous commentary.
524–5 *Ladies Memorandum-book.* 'This day was published . . . (Embellished with . . .
   twelve of the genteelest Head-dresses,) THE LADIES OWN MEMORANDUM BOOK'
   (*Lloyd's Evening Post*, 6–8 January 1773).
526 *side-box* The side-boxes in the theatre rose directly from the side of the
   projecting stage, and so were used for fashionable display by those able to
   afford them.

antiquity by my side as Mr Hardcastle: all I can say will
never argue down a single button from his clothes. I have
often wanted him to throw off his great flaxen wig, and　535
where he was bald, to plaster it over like my Lord Pately,
with powder.

HASTINGS

You are right, madam; for, as among the ladies, there are
none ugly, so among the men there are none old.

MRS HARDCASTLE

But what do you think his answer was? Why, with his usual　540
Gothic vivacity, he said I only wanted him to throw off his
wig to convert it into a *tête* for my own wearing.

HASTINGS

Intolerable! At your age you may wear what you please,
and it must become you.

MRS HARDCASTLE

Pray, Mr Hastings, what do you take to be the most　545
fashionable age about town?

HASTINGS

Some time ago, forty was all the mode; but I'm told the
ladies intend to bring up fifty for the ensuing winter.

MRS HARDCASTLE

Seriously? Then I shall be too young for the fashion.

HASTINGS

No lady begins now to put on jewels till she's past forty.　550
For instance, Miss there, in a polite circle, would be considered as a child, as a mere maker of samplers.

MRS HARDCASTLE

And yet Mrs Niece thinks herself as much a woman, and is
as fond of jewels as the oldest of us all.

HASTINGS

Your niece, is she? And that young gentleman, a brother of　555
yours, I should presume?

MRS HARDCASTLE

My son, sir. They are contracted to each other. Observe
their little sports. They fall in and out ten times a day, as if
they were man and wife already. (*To them*) Well Tony,

---

541 *Gothic* barbarous, unsophisticated (1695)
542 *tête* tall, elaborate hair-piece—'head' (1756)
552 *samplers* pieces of canvas embroidered by young girls as specimens of their skill,
　　usually containing an alphabet and a motto (1523)
553 *Mrs* i.e. 'mistress', synonymous in the eighteenth century with 'miss'
558 *fall ... out* are reconciled (1606) and quarrel (1562) again

child, what soft things are you saying to your cousin Con- 560
stance this evening?

TONY

I have been saying no soft things; but that it's very hard to
be followed about so. Ecod! I've not a place in the house
now that's left to myself but the stable.

MRS HARDCASTLE

Never mind him, Con my dear. He's in another story 565
behind your back.

MISS NEVILLE

There's something generous in my cousin's manner. He
falls out before faces to be forgiven in private.

TONY

That's a damned confounded——crack.

MRS HARDCASTLE

Ah! he's a sly one. Don't you think they're like each other 570
about the mouth, Mr Hastings? The Blenkinsop mouth to
a T. They're of a size too. Back to back, my pretties, that
Mr Hastings may see you. Come Tony.

TONY

You had as good not make me, I tell you.   *Measuring*

MISS NEVILLE

O lud! he has almost cracked my head. 575

MRS HARDCASTLE

Oh the monster! For shame, Tony. You a man, and
behave so!

TONY

If I'm a man, let me have my fortin. Ecod! I'll not be made
a fool of no longer.

MRS HARDCASTLE

Is this, ungrateful boy, all that I'm to get for the pains I 580
have taken in your education? I that have rocked you in
your cradle, and fed that pretty mouth with a spoon! Did
not I work that waistcoat to make you genteel? Did not I
prescribe for you every day, and weep while the receipt was
operating? 585

TONY

Ecod! you had reason to weep, for you have been dosing
me ever since I was born. I have gone through every

569 *crack* lie (1450; obsolete or dialect by 1773)
578 *fortin* fortune
579 *of* L (in 73)
583 *work* 'embroider with a needle' (*SJ*; 1250)
584 *receipt* drug, remedy (1398)

receipt in the *Complete Huswife* ten times over; and you
have thoughts of coursing me through *Quincy* next spring.
But, ecod! I tell you, I'll not be made a fool of no longer.   590

MRS HARDCASTLE
Wasn't it all for your good, viper? Wasn't it all for your
good?

TONY
I wish you'd let me and my good alone then. Snubbing this
way when I'm in spirits. If I'm to have any good, let it come
of itself; not to keep dinging it, dinging it into one so.   595

MRS HARDCASTLE
That's false; I never see you when you're in spirits. No,
Tony, you then go to the alehouse or kennel. I'm never to
be delighted with your agreeable, wild notes, unfeeling
monster!

TONY
Ecod! Mama, your own notes are the wildest of the two.   600

MRS HARDCASTLE
Was ever the like? But I see he wants to break my heart, I
see he does.

HASTINGS
Dear madam, permit me to lecture the young gentleman a
little. I'm certain I can persuade him to his duty.

MRS HARDCASTLE
Well! I must retire. Come, Constance, my love. You see   605
Mr Hastings, the wretchedness of my situation: was ever
poor woman so plagued with a dear, sweet, pretty, provoking, undutiful boy.

Exeunt MRS HARDCASTLE *and* MISS NEVILLE

TONY (*Singing*)
'There was a young man riding by, and fain would have his
will. Rang do didlo dee'. Don't mind her. Let her cry. It's   610
the comfort of her heart. I have seen her and sister cry over
a book for an hour together, and they said, they liked the
book the better the more it made them cry.

HASTINGS
Then you're no friend to the ladies, I find, my pretty
young gentleman?   615

TONY
That's as I find 'em.

588–9 *Complete ... Quincy* the *Compleat Housewife* and John Quincy's *Compleat*
       English Dispensatory were popular home-helps
591 *viper* an allusion to the proverbial phrase 'rearing a viper in one's bosom', used
       to indicate a child's ingratitude to its parents

HASTINGS

Not to her of your mother's choosing, I dare answer? And
yet she appears to me a pretty well-tempered girl.

TONY

That's because you don't know her as well as I. Ecod! I
know every inch about her; and there's not a more bitter   620
cantankerous toad in all Christendom.

HASTINGS (*Aside*)

Pretty encouragement this for a lover!

TONY

I have seen her since the height of that. She has as many
tricks as a hare in a thicket, or a colt the first day's breaking.

HASTINGS

To me she appears sensible and silent!   625

TONY

Ay, before company. But when she's with her playmates
she's as loud as a hog in a gate.

HASTINGS

But there is a meek modesty about her that charms me.

TONY

Yes, but curb her never so little, she kicks up, and you're
flung in a ditch.   630

HASTINGS

Well, but you must allow her a little beauty.—Yes, you
must allow her some beauty.

TONY

Bandbox! She's all a made up thing, mun. Ah! could you
but see Bet Bouncer of these parts, you might then talk of
beauty. Ecod, she has two eyes as black as sloes, and cheeks   635
as broad and red as a pulpit cushion. She'd make two of
she.

HASTINGS

Well, what say you to a friend that would take this bitter
bargain off your hands?

TONY

Anon?   640

HASTINGS

Would you thank him that would take Miss Neville and
leave you to happiness and your dear Betsy?

TONY

Ay; but where is there such a friend, for who would take
her?

633 *Bandbox* showy, trivial (first usage)
640 *Anon?* What did you say? (1723)

HASTINGS

    I am he. If you but assist me, I'll engage to whip her off to 645
France, and you shall never hear more of her.

TONY

    Assist you! Ecod I will, to the last drop of my blood. I'll
clap a pair of horses to your chaise that shall trundle you off
in a twinkling, and maybe get you a part of her fortin
beside, in jewels, that you little dream of. 650

HASTINGS

    My dear Squire, this looks like a lad of spirit.

TONY

    Come along then, and you shall see more of my spirit
before you have done with me. (*Singing*) 'We are the boys
that fears no noise where the thundering cannons roar'.

                                              Exeunt

Act III, Scene i

Enter HARDCASTLE

HARDCASTLE

What could my old friend Sir Charles mean by recommending his son as the modestest young man in town? To me he appears the most impudent piece of brass that ever spoke with a tongue. He has taken possession of the easy chair by the fireside already. He took off his boots in the   5 parlour, and desired me to see them taken care of. I'm desirous to know how his impudence affects my daughter.—She will certainly be shocked at it.

Enter MISS HARDCASTLE, *plainly dressed*

HARDCASTLE

Well, my Kate, I see you have changed your dress as I bid you; and yet, I believe, there was no great occasion.   10

MISS HARDCASTLE

I find such a pleasure, sir, in obeying your commands, that I take care to observe them without ever debating their propriety.

HARDCASTLE

And yet, Kate, I sometimes give you some cause, particularly when I recommended my *modest* gentleman to you as   15 a lover today.

MISS HARDCASTLE

You taught me to expect something extraordinary, and I find the original exceeds the description.

HARDCASTLE

I was never so surprised in my life! He has quite confounded all my faculties!   20

MISS HARDCASTLE

I never saw anything like it: and a man of the world too!

HARDCASTLE

Ay, he learned it all abroad, —what a fool was I, to think a young man could learn modesty by travelling. He might as soon learn wit at a masquerade.

MISS HARDCASTLE

It seems all natural to him.   25

24 *masquerade* a masked ball (1597); Hardcastle is being ironic at the expense of fashionable London

HARDCASTLE

A good deal assisted by bad company and a French
dancing-master.

MISS HARDCASTLE

Sure you mistake, papa! a French dancing-master could
never have taught him that timid look, —that awkward
address, —that bashful manner——   30

HARDCASTLE

Whose look? whose manner? child!

MISS HARDCASTLE

Mr Marlow's: his *mauvaise honte*, his timidity, struck me at
the first sight.

HARDCASTLE

Then your first sight deceived you; for I think him one of
the most brazen first sights that ever astonished my senses.   35

MISS HARDCASTLE

Sure, sir, you rally! I never saw anyone so modest.

HARDCASTLE

And can you be serious! I never saw such a bouncing
swaggering puppy since I was born. Bully Dawson was but
a fool to him.

MISS HARDCASTLE

Surprising! He met me with a respectful bow, a stammer-   40
ing voice, and a look fixed on the ground.

HARDCASTLE

He met me with loud voice, a lordly air, and a familiarity
that froze me to death.

MISS HARDCASTLE

He treated me with diffidence and respect; censured the
manners of the age; admired the prudence of girls that   45
never laughed; tired me with apologies for being tiresome;
then left the room with a bow, and, madam, I would not
for the world detain you.

HARDCASTLE

He spoke to me as if he knew me all his life before. Asked
twenty questions, and never waited for an answer. Inter-   50
rupted my best remarks with some silly pun, and when I
was in my best story of the Duke of Marlborough and
Prince Eugene, he asked if I had not a good hand at making

32 *mauvaise honte* painful self-consciousness (1721)
36 *rally* 'exercise satirical merriment' (*SJ*; 1691)
38 *Bully Dawson* a well-known bully (and coward) of the early eighteenth century
43 *froze ... death* L (made my blood freeze again L)
52–3 *in my ... he asked* 73 (talking of my Friend Bruce, ask'd me L)

punch. Yes, Kate, he asked your father if he was a maker of
punch!   55

MISS HARDCASTLE

One of us must certainly be mistaken.

HARDCASTLE

If he be what he has shown himself, I'm determined he
shall never have my consent.

MISS HARDCASTLE

And if he be the sullen thing I take him, he shall never have
mine.   60

HARDCASTLE

In one thing then we are agreed—to reject him.

MISS HARDCASTLE

Yes. But upon conditions. For if you should find him less
impudent, and I more presuming; if you find him more
respectful, and I more importunate——I don't
know——the fellow is well enough for a man—certainly   65
we don't meet many such at a horse race in the country.

HARDCASTLE

If we should find him so——but that's impossible. The
first appearance has done my business. I'm seldom
deceived in that.

MISS HARDCASTLE

And yet there may be many good qualities under that first   70
appearance.

HARDCASTLE

Ay, when a girl finds a fellow's outside to her taste, she
then sets about guessing the rest of his furniture. With her,
a smooth face stands for good sense, and a genteel figure
for every virtue.   75

MISS HARDCASTLE

I hope, sir, a conversation begun with a compliment to my
good sense won't end with a sneer at my understanding?

HARDCASTLE

Pardon me, Kate. But if young Mr Brazen can find the art
of reconciling contradictions, he may please us both,
perhaps.   80

MISS HARDCASTLE

And as one of us must be mistaken, what if we go to make
further discoveries?

HARDCASTLE

Agreed. But depend on't I'm in the right.

---

73 *furniture* presumably with an obscene implication. L has the more tactful
'qualifications'

MISS HARDCASTLE

And depend on't I'm not much in the wrong.   *Exeunt*

Enter TONY *running in with a Casket*

TONY

Ecod! I have got them. Here they are. My cousin Con's   85
necklaces, bobs and all. My mother shan't cheat the poor
souls out of their fortune neither. Oh! my genus, is that
you?

Enter HASTINGS

HASTINGS

My dear friend, how have you managed with your mother?
I hope you have amused her with pretending love for your   90
cousin, and that you are willing to be reconciled at last?
Our horses will be refreshed in a short time, and we shall
soon be ready to set off.

TONY

And here's something to bear your charges by the way
(*Giving the Casket*). Your sweetheart's jewels. Keep them,   95
and hang those, I say, that would rob you of one of them.

HASTINGS

But how have you procured them from your mother?

TONY

Ask me no questions, and I'll tell you no fibs. I procured
them by the rule of thumb. If I had not a key to every
drawer in mother's bureau, how could I go to the alehouse   100
so often as I do? An honest man may rob himself of his own
at any time.

HASTINGS

Thousands do it every day. But to be plain with you; Miss
Neville is endeavouring to procure them from her aunt this
very instant. If she succeeds, it will be the most delicate   105
way at least of obtaining them.

TONY

Well, keep them, till you know how it will be. But I know
how it will be well enough, she'd as soon part with the only
sound tooth in her head.

HASTINGS

But I dread the effects of her resentment, when she finds   110
she has lost them.

---

86 *bobs* a bob was 'a pendant; an ear-ring' (*SJ*; 1648)
99 *by . . . rule of thumb* by a rough and ready method (1692)—an ironic transference
of meaning

TONY

Never you mind her resentment, leave *me* to manage that. I don't value her resentment the bounce of a cracker. Zounds! here they are. Morris. Prance. *Exit* HASTINGS

Enter MRS HARDCASTLE, MISS NEVILLE

MRS HARDCASTLE

Indeed, Constance, you amaze me. Such a girl as you want   115
jewels? It will be time enough for jewels, my dear, twenty years hence, when your beauty begins to want repairs.

MISS NEVILLE

But what will repair beauty at forty, will certainly improve it at twenty, madam.

MRS HARDCASTLE

Yours, my dear, can admit of none. That natural blush is   120
beyond a thousand ornaments. Besides, child, jewels are quite out at present. Don't you see half the ladies of our acquaintance, my Lady Kill-day-light, and Mrs Crump, and the rest of them, carry their jewels to town, and bring nothing but paste and marcasites back.   125

MISS NEVILLE

But who knows, madam, but somebody that shall be nameless would like me best with all my little finery about me?

MRS HARDCASTLE

Consult your glass, my dear, and then see, if with such a pair of eyes, you want any better sparklers. What do you think, Tony, my dear, does your cousin Con want any   130
jewels, in your eyes, to set off her beauty?

TONY

That's as thereafter may be.

MISS NEVILLE

My dear aunt, if you knew how it would oblige me.

---

113 *bounce of a cracker* the bang (1552) of a firework (1590)
114 *Morris* get out! (1756)
114 *Prance* refers to the rearing of a horse when suddenly spurred into movement: therefore, presumably, 'get a move on' (only usage—metaphoric?)
123 *Lady Kill-day-light* 73c (lady, Kill day light 73a–b)
125 *marcasites* like 'paste', cheap imitation jewels (first usage)

---

123 *Kill-day-light . . . Crump* The lady presumably wastes the day in sleep and the night in revelry; a crump was a hunchback (1698). They take their jewels to Town to pawn them, as Mrs Hardcastle evidently doesn't realize.

MRS HARDCASTLE

A parcel of old-fashioned rose- and table-cut things. They
would make you look like the court of King Solomon at a 135
puppet-show. Besides, I believe I can't readily come at
them. They may be missing for ought I know to the
contrary.

TONY (*Apart to* MRS HARDCASTLE)

Then why don't you tell her so at once, as she's so longing
for them. Tell her they're lost. It's the only way to quiet 140
her. Say they're lost, and call me to bear witness.

MRS HARDCASTLE (*Apart to* TONY)

You know, my dear, I'm only keeping them for you. So if I
say they're gone, you'll bear me witness, will you? He! he!
he!

TONY

Never fear me. Ecod! I'll say I saw them taken out with my 145
own eyes.

MISS NEVILLE

I desire them but for a day, madam. Just to be permitted to
show them as relics, and then they may be locked up again.

MRS HARDCASTLE

To be plain with you, my dear Constance; if I could find
them, you should have them. They're missing, I assure 150
you. Lost, for ought I know; but we must have patience
wherever they are.

MISS NEVILLE

I'll not believe it; this is but a shallow pretence to deny me.
I know they're too valuable to be so slightly kept, and as
you are to answer for the loss. 155

MRS HARDCASTLE

Don't be alarmed, Constance. If they be lost, I must
restore an equivalent. But my son knows they are missing,
and not to be found.

TONY

That I can bear witness to. They are missing, and not to be
found, I'll take my oath on't. 160

MRS HARDCASTLE

You must learn resignation, my dear; for though we lose
our fortune, yet we should not lose our patience. See me,
how calm I am.

---

134 *rose- and table-cut* particular and unfashionable ways of cutting diamonds, with
  few facets
148 *relics* souvenirs, mementos (1601)

MISS NEVILLE

Ay, people are generally calm at the misfortunes of others.

MRS HARDCASTLE

Now, I wonder a girl of your good sense should waste a   165
thought upon such trumpery. We shall soon find them;
and, in the meantime, you shall make use of my garnets till
your jewels be found.

MISS NEVILLE

I detest garnets.

MRS HARDCASTLE

The most becoming things in the world to set off a clear   170
complexion. You have often seen how well they look upon
me. You *shall* have them.   *Exit*

MISS NEVILLE

I dislike them of all things. You shan't stir.—Was ever
anything so provoking to mislay my own jewels, and force
me to wear her trumpery?   175

TONY

Don't be a fool. If she gives you the garnets, take what you
can get. The jewels are your own already. I have stolen
them out of her bureau, and she does not know it. Fly to
your spark, he'll tell you more of the matter. Leave me to
manage *her*.   180

MISS NEVILLE

My dear cousin.   [*Exit*]

TONY

Vanish. She's here, and has missed them already. Zounds!
how she fidgets and spits about like a Catharine wheel.

Enter MRS HARDCASTLE

MRS HARDCASTLE

Confusion! thieves! robbers! We are cheated, plundered,
broke open, undone.   185

TONY

What's the matter, what's the matter, mama? I hope
nothing has happened to any of the good family!

MRS HARDCASTLE

We are robbed. My bureau has been broke open, the jewels
taken out, and I'm undone.

TONY

Oh! is that all? Ha! ha! ha! By the laws, I never saw it   190
better acted in my life. Ecod, I thought you was ruined in
earnest, ha! ha! ha!

167 *garnets* ruby-coloured semi-precious stones: cheap jewelry

MRS HARDCASTLE

Why boy, I *am* ruined in earnest. My bureau has been
broke open, and all taken away.

TONY

Stick to that; ha! ha! ha! Stick to that. I'll bear witness,   195
you know, call me to bear witness.

MRS HARDCASTLE

I tell you, Tony, by all that's precious, the jewels are gone,
and I shall be ruined for ever.

TONY

Sure I know they're gone, and I am to say so.

MRS HARDCASTLE

My dearest Tony, but hear me. They're gone, I say.   200

TONY

By the laws, mama, you make me for to laugh, ha! ha! I
know who took them well enough, ha! ha! ha!

MRS HARDCASTLE

Was there ever such a blockhead, that can't tell the
difference between jest and earnest? I tell you I'm not in
jest, booby.   205

TONY

That's right, that's right: you must be in a bitter passion,
and then nobody will suspect either of us. I'll bear witness
that they are gone.

MRS HARDCASTLE

Was there ever such a cross-grained brute, that won't hear
me! Can you bear witness that you're no better than a fool!   210
Was ever poor woman so beset with fools on one hand, and
thieves on the other?

TONY

I can bear witness to that.

MRS HARDCASTLE

Bear witness again, you blockhead you, and I'll turn you
out of the room directly. My poor niece, what will become   215
of *her*! Do you laugh, you unfeeling brute, as if you
enjoyed my distress?

TONY

I can bear witness to that.

MRS HARDCASTLE

Do you insult me, monster? I'll teach you to vex your
mother, I will.   220

TONY

I can bear witness to that.   *He runs off, she follows him*

221 s.d. *He runs ... him* 73 (Exit. Mrs H. follows, pushing him L)

Enter MISS HARDCASTLE *and* MAID

MISS HARDCASTLE

What an unaccountable creature is that brother of mine, to
send them to the house as an inn, ha! ha! I don't wonder at
his impudence.

MAID

But what is more, madam, the young gentleman, as you   225
passed by in your present dress, asked me, if you were the
barmaid? He mistook you for the barmaid, madam.

MISS HARDCASTLE

Did he? Then as I live I'm resolved to keep up the delu-
sion. Tell me, Pimple, how do you like my present dress?
Don't you think I look something like Cherry in *The Beaux'*   230
Stratagem?

MAID

It's the dress, madam, that every lady wears in the country,
but when she visits or receives company.

MISS HARDCASTLE

And are you sure he does not remember my face or person?

MAID

Certain of it.   235

MISS HARDCASTLE

I vow I thought so; for though we spoke for some time
together, yet his fears were such, that he never once looked
up during the interview. Indeed, if he had, my bonnet
would have kept him from seeing me.

MAID

But what do you hope from keeping him in his mistake?   240

MISS HARDCASTLE

In the first place, I shall be *seen*, and that is no small
advantage to a girl who brings her face to market. Then I
shall perhaps make an acquaintance, and that's no small
victory gained over one who never addresses any but the
wildest of her sex. But my chief aim is to take my gentle- 245
man off his guard, and like an invisible champion of
romance examine the giant's force before I offer to combat.

MAID

But are you sure you can act your part, and disguise your
voice, so that he may mistake that, as he has already
mistaken your person?   250

---

230 *Cherry* was the landlord's daughter in Farquhar's play of 1707. Her wit,
   intelligence, and literacy make her social status ambiguous in that play, and she
   attempts to marry a gentleman, who is himself disguised as a valet.

MISS HARDCASTLE

Never fear me. I think I have got the true bar cant.—Did
your honour call?—Attend the Lion there.——Pipes and
tobacco for the Angel.—The Lamb has been outrageous
this half hour.

MAID

It will do, madam. But he's here.   *Exit* MAID   255

Enter MARLOW

MARLOW

What a bawling in every part of the house; I have scarce a
moment's repose. If I go to the best room, there I find my
host and his story. If I fly to the gallery, there we have my
hostess with her curtsey down to the ground. I have at last
got a moment to myself, and now for recollection.   260

Walks and muses

MISS HARDCASTLE

Did you call, sir? Did your honour call?

MARLOW (*Musing*)

As for Miss Hardcastle, she's too grave and sentimental for
me.

MISS HARDCASTLE

Did your honour call?

She still places herself before him, he turning away

MARLOW

No, child. (*Musing*) Besides from the glimpse I had of her,   265
I think she squints.

MISS HARDCASTLE

I'm sure, sir, I heard the bell ring.

MARLOW

No, no. (*Musing*) I have pleased my father, however, by
coming down, and I'll tomorrow please myself by return-
ing.   270

Taking out his Tablets, and perusing

MISS HARDCASTLE

Perhaps the other gentleman called, sir.

MARLOW

I tell you, no.

MISS HARDCASTLE

I should be glad to know, sir. We have such a parcel of
servants.

252–3 *Lion ... Lamb* rooms in inns were given names.
270 s.d. *Tablets* note-book (first usage)

MARLOW

    No, no, I tell you. (*Looks full in her face*) Yes, child, I think   275
I did call. I wanted——I wanted——I vow, child, you are
vastly handsome.

MISS HARDCASTLE

    O la, sir, you'll make one ashamed.

MARLOW

    Never saw a more sprightly malicious eye. Yes, yes, my
dear, I did call. Have you got any of your—a—what-d'ye-   280
call-it in the house?

MISS HARDCASTLE

    No, sir, we have been out of that these ten days.

MARLOW

    One may call in this house, I find, to very little purpose.
Suppose I should call for a taste, just by way of trial, of the
nectar of your lips; perhaps I might be disappointed of that   285
too.

MISS HARDCASTLE

    Nectar! nectar! that's a liquor there's no call for in these
parts. French, I suppose. We keep no French wines here,
sir.

MARLOW

    Of true English growth, I assure you.   290

MISS HARDCASTLE

    Then it's odd I should not know it. We brew all sorts of
wines in this house, and I have lived here these eighteen
years.

MARLOW

    Eighteen years! Why one would think, child, you kept the
bar before you were born. How old are you?   295

MISS HARDCASTLE

    Oh! sir, I must not tell my age. They say women and music
should never be dated.

MARLOW

    To guess at this distance, you can't be much above forty
(*Approaching*). Yet nearer I don't think so much
(*Approaching*). By coming close to some women they look   300
younger still; but when we come very close indeed
(*Attempting to kiss her*).

---

279 *malicious* mischievous, teasing (1225)

294–8 *Eighteen years . . . forty*. Goldsmith has now cast doubt on the age of all of the
    members of Hardcastle's family except Tony Lumpkin, on whose ambiguous
    age the whole play depends.

MISS HARDCASTLE

Pray, sir, keep your distance. One would think you wanted
to know one's age as they do horses, by mark of mouth.

MARLOW

I protest, child, you use me extremely ill. If you keep me at
this distance, how is it possible you and I can be ever   305
acquainted?

MISS HARDCASTLE

And who wants to be acquainted with you? I want no such
acquaintance, not I. I'm sure you did not treat Miss Hardcastle that was here a while ago in this obstropalous
manner. I'll warrant me, before her you looked dashed,   310
and kept bowing to the ground, and talked, for all the
world, as if you was before a Justice of Peace.

MARLOW (*Aside*)

Egad! she has hit it, sure enough. (*To her*) In awe of her,
child? Ha! ha! ha! A mere, awkward, squinting thing, no,
no. I find you don't know me. I laughed, and rallied her a   315
little; but I was unwilling to be too severe. No, I could not
be too severe, curse me!

MISS HARDCASTLE

Oh! then, sir, you are a favourite, I find, among the ladies?

MARLOW

Yes, my dear, a great favourite. And yet, hang me, I don't
see what they find in me to follow. At the Ladies Club in   320
town, I'm called their agreeable Rattle. Rattle, child, is not
my real name, but one I'm known by. My name is Solomons. Mr Solomons, my dear, at your service.

Offering to salute her

MISS HARDCASTLE

Hold, sir; you were introducing me to your club, not to
yourself. And you're so great a favourite there you say?   325

---

303 *mark of mouth* horse-traders can tell a horse's age from examining its teeth: there
   is a fold in the enamel of the incisor tooth (the 'mark of mouth') that gradually
   disappears with age (1420). Kate is being very rustic
309 *obstropalous* obstreperous (only usage)
321 *Rattle* a 'rattle' was a constant chatterer (1744)
322–3 *My name ... service* 73 (My own name is at your service L)
323 s.d. *salute* kiss (1716)

---

320 *Ladies Club* a fashionable club (to which men were invited) that met in
   Albemarle Street in the 1770s.

MARLOW

Yes, my dear. There's Mrs Mantrap, Lady Betty Blackleg, the Countess of Sligo, Mrs Longhorns, old Miss Biddy Buckskin, and your humble servant, keep up the spirit of the place.

MISS HARDCASTLE

Then it's a very merry place, I suppose.   330

MARLOW

Yes, as merry as cards, suppers, wine, and old women can make us.

MISS HARDCASTLE

And their agreeable Rattle, ha! ha! ha!

MARLOW (*Aside*)

Egad! I don't quite like this chit. She looks knowing, methinks. You laugh, child!   335

MISS HARDCASTLE

I can't but laugh to think what time they all have for minding their work or their family.

MARLOW (*Aside*)

All's well, she don't laugh at me. (*To her*) Do *you* ever work, child?

MISS HARDCASTLE

Ay, sure. There's not a screen or a quilt in the whole house   340
but what can bear witness to that.

MARLOW

Odso! Then you must show me your embroidery. I embroider and draw patterns myself a little. If you want a judge of your work you must apply to me.

Seizing her hand

MISS HARDCASTLE

Ay, but the colours don't look well by candlelight. You   345
shall see all in the morning.   *Struggling*

MARLOW

And why not now, my angel? Such beauty fires beyond the power of resistance.——Pshaw! the father here! My old

---

326 *Mantrap ... Blackleg* a man-trap was a vicious toothed gin-trap, used against
poachers (first usage); and a black-leg was a card-sharper (1771)
327 *Longhorns* L (Langhorns 73)

327–8 *Biddy Buckskin* (Rachael Buckskin in L) referring to Rachel Lloyd, one of
the leading lights of the club.

luck: I never nicked seven that I did not throw ames ace
three times following.   *Exit* MARLOW   350

Enter HARDCASTLE, *who stands in surprise*

HARDCASTLE

So, madam! So I find *this* is your *modest* lover. This is your
humble admirer that kept his eyes fixed on the ground, and
only adored at humble distance. Kate, Kate, art thou not
ashamed to deceive thy father so?

MISS HARDCASTLE

Never trust me, dear papa, but he's still the modest man I   355
first took him for, you'll be convinced of it as well as I.

HARDCASTLE

By the hand of my body I believe his impudence is infect-
ious! Didn't I see him seize your hand? Didn't I see him
haul you about like a milkmaid? and now you talk of his
respect and his modesty, forsooth!   360

MISS HARDCASTLE

But if I shortly convince you of his modesty, that he has
only the faults that will pass off with time, and the virtues
that will improve with age, I hope you'll forgive him.

HARDCASTLE

The girl would actually make one run mad! I tell you I'll
not be convinced. I am convinced. He has scarcely been   365
three hours in the house, and he has already encroached on
all my prerogatives. You may like his impudence, and call
it modesty. But my son-in-law, madam, must have very
different qualifications.

MISS HARDCASTLE

Sir, I ask but this night to convince you.   370

HARDCASTLE

You shall not have half the time, for I have thoughts of
turning him out this very hour.

MISS HARDCASTLE

Give me that hour then, and I hope to satisfy you.

HARDCASTLE

Well, an hour let it be then. But I'll have no trifling with
your father. All fair and open, do you mind me?   375

---

349 *nicked seven ... ames ace* Marlow is talking about dice: he never made the
   winning throw without then three times throwing the lowest possible score,
   with both dice showing one
354 *thy* L (your 73)

MISS HARDCASTLE

I hope, sir, you have ever found that I considered your commands as my pride; for your kindness is such, that my duty as yet has been inclination.   *Exeunt*

Act IV, Scene i

Enter HASTINGS *and* MISS NEVILLE

HASTINGS
You surprise me! Sir Charles Marlow expected here this
night? Where have you had your information?
MISS NEVILLE
You may depend upon it. I just saw his letter to Mr
Hardcastle, in which he tells him he intends setting out a
few hours after his son.   5
HASTINGS
Then, my Constance, all must be completed before he
arrives. He knows me; and should he find me here, would
discover my name, and perhaps my designs, to the rest of
the family.
MISS NEVILLE
The jewels, I hope, are safe.   10
HASTINGS
Yes, yes. I have sent them to Marlow, who keeps the keys
of our baggage. In the meantime, I'll go to prepare matters
for our elopement. I have had the Squire's promise of a
fresh pair of horses; and, if I should not see him again, will
write him further directions.   *Exit*   15
MISS NEVILLE
Well! success attend you. In the meantime, I'll go amuse
my aunt with the old pretence of a violent passion for my
cousin.   *Exit*

Enter MARLOW, *followed by a* SERVANT

MARLOW
I wonder what Hastings could mean by sending me so
valuable a thing as a casket to keep for him, when he knows 20
the only place I have is the seat of a post-coach at an
inn-door. Have you deposited the casket with the landlady,
as I ordered you? Have you put it into her own hands?
SERVANT
Yes, your honour.
MARLOW
She said she'd keep it safe, did she?   25
SERVANT
Yes, she said she'd keep it safe enough; she asked me, how

I came by it? and she said she had a great mind to make me
give an account of myself.   *Exit* SERVANT

MARLOW

Ha! ha! ha! They're safe however. What an unaccountable
set of beings have we got amongst! This little barmaid   30
though runs in my head most strangely, and drives out the
absurdities of all the rest of the family. She's mine, she
must be mine, or I'm greatly mistaken.

Enter HASTINGS

HASTINGS

Bless me! I quite forgot to tell her that I intended to
prepare at the bottom of the garden. Marlow here, and in   35
spirits too!

MARLOW

Give me joy, George! Crown me, shadow me with laurels!
Well, George, after all, we modest fellows don't want for
success among the women.

HASTINGS

Some women you mean. But what success has your   40
honour's modesty been crowned with now, that it grows so
insolent upon us?

MARLOW

Didn't you see the tempting, brisk, lovely, little thing that
runs about the house with a bunch of keys to its girdle?

HASTINGS

Well! and what then?   45

MARLOW

She's mine, you rogue you. Such fire, such motion, such
eyes, such lips——but, egad! she would not let me kiss
them though.

HASTINGS

But are you so sure, so very sure of her?

MARLOW

Why man, she talked of showing me her work above-stairs,   50
and I am to improve the pattern.

HASTINGS

But how can *you*, Charles, go about to rob a woman of her
honour?

MARLOW

Pshaw! pshaw! we all know the honour of the barmaid of
an inn. I don't intend to *rob* her, take my word for it, there's   55
nothing in this house, I shan't honestly *pay* for.

50 *above-stairs* upstairs (1758); i.e. in her bedroom

HASTINGS

I believe the girl has virtue.

MARLOW

And if she has, I should be the last man in the world that would attempt to corrupt it.

HASTINGS

You have taken care, I hope, of the casket I sent you to lock   60
up? It's in safety?

MARLOW

Yes, yes. It's safe enough. I have taken care of it. But how could you think the seat of a post-coach at an inn-door a place of safety? Ah! numbskull! I have taken better precautions for you than you did for yourself.————I   65
have————

HASTINGS

What!

MARLOW

I have sent it to the landlady to keep for you.

HASTINGS

To the landlady!

MARLOW

The landlady.   70

HASTINGS

You did.

MARLOW

I did. She's to be answerable for its forthcoming, you know.

HASTINGS

Yes, she'll bring it forth, with a witness.

MARLOW

Wasn't I right? I believe you'll allow that I acted prudently   75
upon this occasion?

HASTINGS (*Aside*)

He must not see my uneasiness.

MARLOW

You seem a little disconcerted though, methinks. Sure nothing has happened?

HASTINGS

No, nothing. Never was in better spirits in all my life. And   80
so you left it with the landlady who, no doubt, very readily undertook the charge?

MARLOW

Rather too readily. For she not only kept the casket; but,

74 *with a witness* with a vengeance, without a doubt (1575)

through her great precaution, was going to keep the
messenger too. Ha! ha! ha!   85

HASTINGS

He! he! he! They're safe however.

MARLOW

As a guinea in a miser's purse.

HASTINGS (*Aside*)

So now all hopes of fortune are at an end, and we must set
off without it. (*To him*) Well, Charles, I'll leave you to your
meditations on the pretty barmaid, and, he! he! he! may   90
you be as successful for yourself as you have been for me.

Exit

MARLOW

Thank ye, George! I ask no more. Ha! ha! ha!

Enter HARDCASTLE

HARDCASTLE

I no longer know my own house. It's turned all topsy-
turvy. His servants have got drunk already. I'll bear it no
longer, and yet, from my respect for his father, I'll be calm.   95
(*To him*) Mr Marlow, your servant, I'm your very humble
servant.   *Bowing low*

MARLOW

Sir, your humble servant. (*Aside*) What's to be the wonder
now?

HARDCASTLE

I believe, sir, you must be sensible, sir, that no man alive   100
ought to be more welcome than your father's son, sir. I
hope you think so?

MARLOW

I do from my soul, sir. I don't want much entreaty. I
generally make my father's son welcome wherever he goes.

HARDCASTLE

I believe you do, from my soul, sir. But though I say   105
nothing to your own conduct, that of your servants is
insufferable. Their manner of drinking is setting a very
bad example in this house, I assure you.

MARLOW

I protest, my very good sir, that's no fault of mine. If they
don't drink as they ought *they* are to blame. I ordered them   110
not to spare the cellar. I did, I assure you. (*To the Side
Scene*) Here, let one of my servants come up. (*To him*) My

111 *assure you* L, 73d (assure 73a–c)

positive directions were, that as I did not drink myself,
they should make up for my deficiencies below.

HARDCASTLE

Then they had your orders for what they do! I'm satisfied! 115

MARLOW

They had, I assure you. You shall hear from one of themselves.

Enter SERVANT *drunk*

MARLOW

You, Jeremy! Come forward, sirrah! What were my
orders? Were you not told to drink freely, and call for what
you thought fit, for the good of the house? 120

HARDCASTLE (*Aside*)

I begin to lose my patience.

SERVANT

Please your honour, liberty and Fleet Street for ever!
Though I'm but a servant, I'm as good as another man. I'll
drink for no man before supper, sir, damme! Good liquor
will sit upon a good supper, but a good supper will not sit 125
upon——hiccup——upon my conscience, sir.

MARLOW

You see, my old friend, the fellow is as drunk as he can
possibly be. I don't know what you'd have more, unless
you'd have the poor devil soused in a beer-barrel.

HARDCASTLE

Zounds! He'll drive me distracted if I contain myself any 130
longer. Mr Marlow, sir; I have submitted to your insolence
for more than four hours, and I see no likelihood of its
coming to an end. I'm now resolved to be master here, sir,
and I desire that you and your drunken pack may leave my
house directly. 135

MARLOW

Leave your house!——Sure you jest, my good friend?
What, when I'm doing what I can to please you?

HARDCASTLE

I tell you, sir, you don't please me; so I desire you'll leave
my house.

---

122 *liberty and Fleet Street for ever!* What Jeremy means has never been satisfactor-
ily resolved. Fleet Street was not yet a synonym for the Press. He is either
giving voice to, or parodying, a partisan's cry from the Wilkes riots, like 'Wilkes
and Liberty'. 'Fleet Street' may symbolize the metropolis, since it was a
particularly busy and vital street, or may only refer to the fact that it contained,
in the eighteenth century, 37 taverns.

MARLOW

Sure you cannot be serious? At this time o'night, and such   140
a night. You only mean to banter me?

HARDCASTLE

I tell you, sir, I'm serious; and, now that my passions are
roused, I say this house is mine, sir; this house is mine, and
I command you to leave it directly.

MARLOW

Ha! ha! ha! A puddle in a storm. I shan't stir a step, I   145
assure you. (*In a serious tone*) This, your house, fellow! It's
my house. This is my house. Mine, while I choose to stay.
What right have you to bid me leave this house, sir? I never
met with such impudence, curse me, never in my whole
life before.   150

HARDCASTLE

Nor I, confound me if ever I did. To come to my house, to
call for what he likes, to turn me out of my own chair, to
insult the family, to order his servants to get drunk, and
then to tell me, 'This house is mine, sir'. By all that's
impudent it makes me laugh. Ha! ha! ha! Pray, sir, (*Ban-*   155
tering) as you take the house, what think you of taking the
rest of the furniture? There's a pair of silver candlesticks,
and there's a firescreen, and here's a pair of brazen-nosed
bellows, perhaps you may take a fancy to them?

MARLOW

Bring me your bill, sir, bring me your bill, and let's make   160
no more words about it.

HARDCASTLE

There are a set of prints too. What think you of the *Rake's
Progress* for your own apartment?

MARLOW

Bring me your bill, I say; and I'll leave you and your
infernal house directly.   165

HARDCASTLE

Then there's a mahogany table, that you may see your own
face in.

MARLOW

My bill, I say.

HARDCASTLE

I had forgot the great chair, for your own particular slum-
bers, after a hearty meal.   170

MARLOW

Zounds! bring me my bill, I say, and let's hear no more
on't.

HARDCASTLE

Young man, young man, from your father's letter to me, I
was taught to expect a well-bred modest man as a visitor
here, but now I find him no better than a coxcomb and a   175
bully; but he will be down here presently, and shall hear
more of it.   *Exit*

MARLOW

How's this! Sure I have not mistaken the house! Everything looks like an inn. The servants cry, 'Coming'. The
attendance is awkward; the barmaid too to attend us. But   180
she's here, and will further inform me. Whither so fast,
child? A word with you.

Enter MISS HARDCASTLE

MISS HARDCASTLE

Let it be short then. I'm in a hurry. (*Aside*) I believe he
begins to find out his mistake, but it's too soon quite to
undeceive him.   185

MARLOW

Pray, child, answer me one question. What are you, and
what may your business in this house be?

MISS HARDCASTLE

A relation of the family, sir.

MARLOW

What? A poor relation?

MISS HARDCASTLE

Yes, sir. A poor relation appointed to keep the keys, and to   190
see that the guests want nothing in my power to give them.

MARLOW

That is, you act as the barmaid of this inn.

MISS HARDCASTLE

Inn! O law—What brought that in your head? One of the
best families in the county keep an inn! Ha! ha! ha! old Mr
Hardcastle's house an inn!   195

MARLOW

Mr Hardcastle's house! Is this Mr Hardcastle's house,
child!

MISS HARDCASTLE

Ay, sure. Whose else should it be?

MARLOW

So then all's out, and I have been damnably imposed on.   200
Oh, confound my stupid head, I shall be laughed at over

196 *this* L (this house 73)

the whole town. I shall be stuck up in *caricatura* in all the
print-shops. The *Dullissimo Macaroni*. To mistake this
house of all others for an inn, and my father's old friend for
an inn-keeper. What a swaggering puppy must he take me
for! What a silly puppy do I find myself! There again, may   205
I be hanged, my dear, but I mistook you for the barmaid.

MISS HARDCASTLE

Dear me! dear me! I'm sure there's nothing in my
behaviour to put me upon a level with one of that stamp.

MARLOW

Nothing, my dear, nothing. But I was in for a list of
blunders, and could not help making you a subscriber. My   210
stupidity saw everything the wrong way. I mistook your
assiduity for assurance, and your simplicity for allure-
ment. But it's over—This house I no more show *my* face
in.

MISS HARDCASTLE

I hope, sir, I have done nothing to disoblige you. I'm sure I   215
should be sorry to affront any gentleman who has been so
polite, and said so many civil things to me. I'm sure I
should be sorry (*Pretending to cry*) if he left the family upon
my account. I'm sure I should be sorry people said anything amiss, since I have no fortune but my character.   220

MARLOW (*Aside*)

By heaven, she weeps. This is the first mark of tenderness I
ever had from a modest woman, and it touches me; (*To
her*) excuse me, my lovely girl, you are the only part of the
family I leave with reluctance. But to be plain with you, the
difference of our birth, fortune, and education, make an   225
honourable connection impossible; and I can never har-
bour a thought of seducing simplicity that trusted in my
honour, or bringing ruin upon one, whose only fault was
being too lovely.

MISS HARDCASTLE (*Aside*)

Generous man! I now begin to admire him. (*To him*) But   230
I'm sure my family is as good as Miss Hardcastle's, and

---

208 *behaviour* behaviour. Kate is mispronouncing an 'unfamiliar' and (for a barmaid) 'elegant' word
222 *touches me* 73 (touches me. How natural it is for a Recluse to fall in love at first.
L)

201–2 *stuck up . . . Macaroni*. A macaroni was a fop, a dandy (1764). Marlow is afraid
that if the word gets back to London, he will be included in a popular series of
caricatures that particularly attacked dandyism.

though I'm poor, that's no great misfortune to a contented
mind, and, until this moment, I never thought that it was
bad to want fortune.

MARLOW

And why now, my pretty simplicity?   235

MISS HARDCASTLE

Because it puts me at a distance from one, that if I had a
thousand pound I would give it all too.

MARLOW (*Aside*)

This simplicity bewitches me, so that if I stay I'm undone.
I must make one bold effort, and leave her. (*To her*) Your
partiality in my favour, my dear, touches me most sens-   240
ibly, and were I to live for myself alone, I could easily fix
my choice. But I owe too much to the opinion of the world,
too much to the authority of a father, so that—I can
scarcely speak it—it affects me. Farewell.   *Exit*

MISS HARDCASTLE

I never knew half his merit till now. He shall not go, if I   245
have power or art to detain him. I'll still preserve the
character in which I stooped to conquer, but will undeceive my papa, who, perhaps, may laugh him out of his
resolution.   *Exit*

Enter TONY, MISS NEVILLE

TONY

Ay, you may steal for yourselves the next time. I have done   250
my duty. She has got the jewels again, that's a sure thing;
but she believes it was all a mistake of the servants.

MISS NEVILLE

But, my dear cousin, sure you won't forsake us in this
distress? If she in the least suspects that I am going off, I
shall certainly be locked up, or sent to my aunt Pedigree's,   255
which is ten times worse.

TONY

To be sure, aunts of all kinds are damned bad things. But
what can I do? I have got you a pair of horses that will fly
like Whistlejacket, and I'm sure you can't say but I have
courted you nicely before her face. Here she comes, we   260
must court a bit or two more, for fear she should suspect
us.   *They retire, and seem to fondle*

Enter MRS HARDCASTLE

---

232 *though* 73 (I'm not behind her in Plain-work and Pastry. What tho' L)
259 *Whistlejacket* a famous racehorse, that won races in the mid-1750s

MRS HARDCASTLE

Well, I was greatly fluttered, to be sure. But my son tells
me it was all a mistake of the servants. I shan't be easy,
however, till they are fairly married, and then let her keep   265
her own fortune. But what do I see! Fondling together, as
I'm alive. I never saw Tony so sprightly before. Ah! have I
caught you, my pretty doves! What, billing, exchanging
stolen glances, and broken murmurs? Ah!

TONY

As for murmurs, mother, we grumble a little now and   270
then, to be sure. But there's no love lost between us.

MRS HARDCASTLE

A mere sprinkling, Tony, upon the flame, only to make it
burn brighter.

MISS NEVILLE

Cousin Tony promises to give us more of his company at
home. Indeed, he shan't leave us any more. It won't leave   275
us cousin Tony, will it?

TONY

Oh! it's a pretty creature. No, I'd sooner leave a hare in her
form, the dogs in full cry, or my horse in a pound, than
leave you when you smile upon one so. Your laugh makes
you so becoming.   280

MISS NEVILLE

Agreeable cousin! Who can help admiring that natural
humour, that pleasant, broad, red, thoughtless, (*Patting
his cheek*) ah! it's a bold face.

MRS HARDCASTLE

Pretty innocence.

TONY

I'm sure I always loved cousin Con's hazel eyes, and her   285
pretty long fingers, that she twists this way and that, over
the haspicholls, like a parcel of bobbins.

277–8 *a hare ... cry, or* L (om. 73)

287 *haspicholls* harpsichord: a Lumpkinism

287 *bobbins* spindles carrying thread, that were allowed to dangle and dance about
during lace-making (1530)

271 *no love lost* Goldsmith coined this phrase. Its modern usage has the ironic,
opposite meaning to the literal one; both, of course, are intended here, but
primarily the literal one.

MRS HARDCASTLE

Ah, he would charm the bird from the tree. I was never so happy before. My boy takes after his father, poor Mr Lumpkin, exactly. The jewels, my dear Con, shall be yours incontinently. You shall have them. Isn't he a sweet boy, my dear? You shall be married tomorrow, and we'll put off the rest of his education, like Dr Drowsy's sermons, to a fitter opportunity.   290

Enter DIGGORY

DIGGORY

Where's the Squire? I have got a letter for your worship.   295

TONY

Give it to my mama. She reads all my letters first.

DIGGORY

I had orders to deliver it into your own hands.

TONY

Who does it come from?

DIGGORY

Your worship mun ask that o' the letter itself.

TONY

I could wish to know, though.   300
                    Turning the letter, and gazing on it

MISS NEVILLE (*Aside*)

Undone, undone. A letter to him from Hastings. I know the hand. If my aunt sees it, we are ruined for ever. I'll keep her employed a little if I can. (*To* MRS HARDCASTLE) But I have not told you, madam, of my cousin's smart answer just now to Mr Marlow. We so laughed— You   305
must know, madam—this way a little, for he must not hear us.   *They confer*

TONY (*Still gazing*)

A damned cramp piece of penmanship, as ever I saw in my life. I can read your print-hand very well. But here there are such handles, and shanks, and dashes, that one can   310
scarce tell the head from the tail. 'To Anthony Lumpkin, Esquire'. It's very odd, I can read the outside of my letters, where my own name is, well enough. But when I come to open it, it's all—buzz. That's hard, very hard; for the inside of the letter is always the cream of the correspon-   315
dence.

MRS HARDCASTLE

Ha! ha! ha! Very well, very well. And so my son was too hard for the philosopher.

MISS NEVILLE

Yes, madam; but you must hear the rest, madam. A little
more this way, or he may hear us. You'll hear how he   320
puzzled him again.

MRS HARDCASTLE

He seems strangely puzzled now himself, methinks.

TONY (*Still gazing*)

A damned up and down hand, as if it was disguised in
liquor. (*Reading*) 'Dear Squire'. Ay, that's that. Then
there's an 'M', and a 'T', and an 'S', but whether the next be   325
an 'izzard' or an 'R', confound me, I cannot tell.

MRS HARDCASTLE

What's that, my dear? Can I give you any assistance?

MISS NEVILLE

Pray, aunt, let me read it. Nobody reads a cramp hand
better than I. (*Twitching the letter from her*) Do you know
who it is from?   330

TONY

Can't tell, except from Dick Ginger the feeder.

MISS NEVILLE

Ay, so it is, (*Pretending to read*) 'Dear Squire, Hoping that
you're in health, as I am at this present. The gentlemen of
the Shake-bag club has cut the gentlemen of Goose-green
quite out of feather. The odds—um—odd battle—   335
um—long fighting'—um—here, here, it's all about cocks,
and fighting; it's of no consequence, here, put it up, put it
up.

Thrusting the crumpled letter upon him

TONY

But I tell you, Miss, it's of all the consequence in the world.
I would not lose the rest of it for a guinea. Here, mother, do   340
you make it out. Of no consequence!

Giving MRS HARDCASTLE *the letter*

MRS HARDCASTLE

How's this! (*Reads*) 'Dear Squire, I'm now waiting for
Miss Neville, with a post-chaise and pair, at the bottom of
the garden, but I find my horses yet unable to perform the
journey. I expect you'll assist us with a pair of fresh horses,   345

---

324 *Squire* L (*Sir* 73)

326 *izzard* Z (1738)

331 *feeder* trainer of fighting-cocks (first usage)

334 *Shake-bag club* a shake-bag was a large fighting-cock (1709)

334 *Goose-green* i.e. the cock's colour (originally 'goose-turd green')

335 *odd battle* uneven match? (not in *OED*)

as you promised. Dispatch is necessary, as the *hag* (ay the hag) your mother, will otherwise suspect us. Yours, Hastings. Grant me patience! I shall run distracted! My rage chokes me!

MISS NEVILLE

I hope, madam, you'll suspend your resentment for a few 350
moments, and not impute to me any impertinence, or sinister design that belongs to another.

MRS HARDCASTLE (*Curtseying very low*)

Fine spoken, madam, you are most miraculously polite and engaging, and quite the very pink of courtesy and circumspection, madam. (*Changing her tone*) And you, you 355
great ill-fashioned oaf with scarce sense enough to keep your mouth shut. Were you too joined against me? But I'll defeat all your plots in a moment. As for you, madam, since you have got a pair of fresh horses ready, it would be cruel to disappoint them. So, if you please, instead of 360
running away with your spark, prepare, this very moment, to run off with *me*. Your old aunt Pedigree will keep you secure, I'll warrant me. You too, sir, may mount your horse, and guard us upon the way. Here, Thomas, Roger, Diggory. I'll show you that I wish you better than you do 365
yourselves.   *Exit*

MISS NEVILLE

So now I'm completely ruined.

TONY

Ay, that's a sure thing.

MISS NEVILLE

What better could be expected from being connected with such a stupid fool, and after all the nods and signs I made 370
him.

TONY

By the laws, Miss, it was your own cleverness, and not my stupidity, that did your business. You were so nice and so busy with your Shake-bags and Goose-greens, that I thought you could never be making believe.   375

Enter HASTINGS

HASTINGS

So, sir, I find by my servant, that you have shown my letter, and betrayed us. Was this well done, young gentleman?

373 *nice* 'superfluously exact. It is often used to express a culpable delicacy' (*SJ*; 1589)

TONY

   Here's another. Ask Miss there who betrayed you. Ecod, it
   was her doing, not mine.   380

                    Enter MARLOW

MARLOW

   So I have been finely used here among you. Rendered
   contemptible, driven into ill manners, despised, insulted,
   laughed at.

TONY

   Here's another. We shall have old Bedlam broke loose
   presently.   385

MISS NEVILLE

   And there, sir, is the gentleman to whom we all owe every
   obligation.

MARLOW

   What can I say to him, a mere boy, an idiot, whose ignorance and age are a protection?

HASTINGS

   A poor contemptible booby, that would but disgrace cor-   390
   rection.

MISS NEVILLE

   Yet with cunning and malice enough to make himself
   merry with all our embarrassments.

HASTINGS

   An insensible cub.

MARLOW

   Replete with tricks and mischief.   395

TONY

   Baw! damme, but I'll fight you both one after the
   other,——with baskets.

MARLOW

   As for him, he's below resentment. But your conduct, Mr
   Hastings, requires an explanation. You knew of my mistakes, yet would not undeceive me.   400

HASTINGS

   Tortured as I am with my own disappointments, is this a
   time for explanations! It is not friendly, Mr Marlow.

MARLOW

   But, sir—

390–1 *protection* ... *correction* euphemisms: they mean that he is too young to
   challenge to a duel
397 *baskets* single-sticks with protective basket-hilts (first usage). Presumably the
   dash indicates that the gentlemen half-draw their swords at this point

MISS NEVILLE

Mr Marlow, we never kept on your mistake, till it was too
late to undeceive you. Be pacified.   405

Enter SERVANT

SERVANT

My mistress desires you'll get ready immediately, madam.
The horses are putting to. Your hat and things are in the
next room. We are to go thirty miles before morning.
Exit SERVANT

MISS NEVILLE

Well, well; I'll come presently.

MARLOW (*To* HASTINGS)

Was it well done, sir, to assist in rendering me ridiculous?   410
To hang me out for the scorn of all my acquaintance?
Depend upon it, sir, I shall expect an explanation.

HASTINGS

Was it well done, sir, if you're upon that subject, to deliver
what I entrusted to yourself, to the care of another, sir?

MISS NEVILLE

Mr Hastings, Mr Marlow. Why will you increase my dis-   415
tress by this groundless dispute? I implore, I entreat
you——

Enter SERVANT

SERVANT

Your cloak, madam. My mistress is impatient.

MISS NEVILLE

I come. Pray be pacified. If I leave you thus, I shall die
with apprehension.   420

SERVANT

Your fan, muff, and gloves, madam. The horses are waiting.

MISS NEVILLE

Oh, Mr Marlow! if you knew what a scene of constraint
and ill-nature lies before me, I'm sure it would convert
your resentment into pity.   425

MARLOW

I'm so distracted with a variety of passions, that I don't
know what I do. Forgive me, madam. George, forgive me.
You know my hasty temper, and should not exasperate it.

409 *presently* 'immediately' (*SJ*; 1430)
420 *apprehension.* L (apprehension. Enter SERVANT 73)

HASTINGS

The torture of my situation is my only excuse.

MISS NEVILLE

Well, my dear Hastings, if you have that esteem for me that   430
I think, that I am sure you have, your constancy for three
years will but increase the happiness of our future connection. If—

MRS HARDCASTLE (*Within*)

Miss Neville! Constance, why Constance, I say.

MISS NEVILLE

I'm coming. Well, constancy. Remember, constancy is the   435
word.   *Exit*

HASTINGS

My heart! How can I support this? To be so near happiness, and such happiness.

MARLOW (*To* TONY)

You see now, young gentleman, the effects of your folly.
What might be amusement to you, is here disappointment,   440
and even distress.

TONY (*From a reverie*)

Ecod, I have hit it. It's here. Your hands. Yours and yours,
my poor Sulky. My boots there, ho! Meet me two hours
hence at the bottom of the garden; and if you don't find
Tony Lumpkin a more good-natured fellow than you   445
thought for, I'll give you leave to run me through the guts
with a shoulder of mutton. Come along. My boots, ho!

Exeunt

446–7 *run ... mutton* L (take my best horse and Bet Bouncer into the bargain 73)

442–3 *Yours ... Sulky* presumably a quotation, but no one knows where from.

Act V, Scene i

Scene Continues

Enter HASTINGS *and* SERVANT

HASTINGS
You saw the old lady and Miss Neville drive off, you say.
SERVANT
Yes, your honour. They went off in a post coach, and the young Squire went on horseback. They're thirty miles off by this time.
HASTINGS
Then all my hopes are over.   5
SERVANT
Yes, sir. Old Sir Charles is arrived. He and the old gentleman of the house have been laughing at Mr Marlow's mistake this half hour. They are coming this way.
HASTINGS
Then I must not be seen. So now to my fruitless appointment at the bottom of the garden. This is about the time.   10
Exeunt

Enter SIR CHARLES *and* HARDCASTLE

HARDCASTLE
Ha! ha! ha! The peremptory tone in which he sent forth his sublime commands.
SIR CHARLES
And the reserve with which I suppose he treated all your advances.
HARDCASTLE
And yet he might have seen something in me above a   15
common inn-keeper, too.
SIR CHARLES
Yes, Dick, but he mistook you for an uncommon inn-keeper, ha! ha! ha!
HARDCASTLE
Well, I'm in too good spirits to think of anything but joy.
Yes, my dear friend, this union of our families will make   20
our personal friendship hereditary; and though my daughter's fortune is but small——
SIR CHARLES
Why, Dick, will you talk of fortune to *me*? My son is

21 *friendship* L (friendships 73)

possessed of more than a competence already, and can
want nothing but a good and virtuous girl to share his　25
happiness and increase it. If they like each other, as you say
they do——

HARDCASTLE

If, man? I tell you they *do* like each other. My daughter as
good as told me so.

SIR CHARLES

But girls are apt to flatter themselves, you know.　30

HARDCASTLE

I saw him grasp her hand in the warmest manner myself;
and here he comes to put you out of your 'ifs', I warrant
him.

Enter MARLOW

MARLOW

I come, sir, once more, to ask pardon for my strange
conduct. I can scarce reflect on my insolence without　35
confusion.

HARDCASTLE

Tut, boy, a trifle. You take it too gravely. An hour or two's
laughing with my daughter will set all to rights again.
She'll never like you the worse for it.

MARLOW

Sir, I shall be always proud of her approbation.　40

HARDCASTLE

Approbation is but a cold word, Mr Marlow; if I am not
deceived, you have something more than approbation
thereabouts. You take me.

MARLOW

Really, sir, I have not that happiness.

HARDCASTLE

Come, boy, I'm an old fellow, and know what's what, as　45
well as you that are younger. I know what has passed
between you; but mum.

MARLOW

Sure, sir, nothing has passed between us but the most
profound respect on my side, and the most distant reserve
on hers. You don't think, sir, that my impudence has been　50
passed upon all the rest of the family?

HARDCASTLE

Impudence! No, I don't say that—Not quite impudence—Though girls like to be played with, and rumpled

52 s.p. HARDCASTLE L (MISS HARDCASTLE 73)

a little too sometimes. But she has told no tales, I assure
you.   55

MARLOW

I never gave her the slightest cause.

HARDCASTLE

Well, well, I like modesty in its place well enough. But this
is over-acting, young gentleman. You *may* be open. Your
father and I will like you the better for it.

MARLOW

May I die, sir, if I ever——   60

HARDCASTLE

I tell you, she don't dislike you; and as I'm sure you like
her——

MARLOW

Dear sir—I protest, sir——

HARDCASTLE

I see no reason why you should not be joined as fast as the
parson can tie you.   65

MARLOW

But hear me, sir——

HARDCASTLE

Your father approves the match, I admire it, every
moment's delay will be doing mischief, so——

MARLOW

But why won't you hear me? By all that's just and true, I
never gave Miss Hardcastle the slightest mark of my   70
attachment, or even the most distant hint to suspect me of
affection. We had but one interview, and that was formal,
modest, and uninteresting.

HARDCASTLE (*Aside*)

This fellow's formal modest impudence is beyond bearing.

SIR CHARLES

And you never grasped her hand, or made any protesta-   75
tions!

MARLOW

As heaven is my witness, I came down in obedience to your
commands. I saw the lady without emotion, and parted
without reluctance. I hope you'll exact no further proofs of
my duty, nor prevent me from leaving a house in which I   80
suffer so many mortifications.   *Exit*

SIR CHARLES

I'm astonished at the air of sincerity with which he parted.

HARDCASTLE

And I'm astonished at the deliberate intrepidity of his
assurance.

SIR CHARLES
I dare pledge my life and honour upon his truth.   85
HARDCASTLE
Here comes my daughter, and I would stake my happiness
upon her veracity.

Enter MISS HARDCASTLE

HARDCASTLE
Kate, come hither, child. Answer us sincerely, and with-
out reserve; has Mr Marlow made you any professions of
love and affection.   90
MISS HARDCASTLE
The question is very abrupt, sir! But since you require
unreserved sincerity, I think he has.
HARDCASTLE (*To* SIR CHARLES)
You see.
SIR CHARLES
And pray, madam, have you and my son had more than
one interview?   95
MISS HARDCASTLE
Yes, sir, several.
HARDCASTLE (*To* SIR CHARLES)
You see.
SIR CHARLES
But did he profess any attachment?
MISS HARDCASTLE
A lasting one.
SIR CHARLES
Did he talk of love?   100
MISS HARDCASTLE
Much, sir.
SIR CHARLES
Amazing! And all this formally?
MISS HARDCASTLE
Formally.
HARDCASTLE
Now, my friend, I hope you are satisfied.
SIR CHARLES
And how did he behave, madam?   105
MISS HARDCASTLE
As most professed admirers do. Said some civil things of
my face, talked much of his want of merit, and the great-
ness of mine; mentioned his heart, gave a short tragedy
speech, and ended with pretended rapture.

SIR CHARLES

Now I'm perfectly convinced, indeed. I know his conver-   110
sation among women to be modest and submissive. This
forward canting ranting manner by no means describes
him, and I am confident, he never sat for the picture.

MISS HARDCASTLE

Then what, sir, if I should convince you to your face of my
sincerity? If you and my papa, in about half an hour, will   115
place yourselves behind that screen, you shall hear him
declare his passion to me in person.

SIR CHARLES

Agreed. And if I find him what you describe, all my
happiness in him must have an end.   *Exit*

MISS HARDCASTLE

And if you don't find him what I describe—I fear my   120
happiness must never have a beginning.   *Exeunt*

Act V, Scene ii

Scene changes to the Back of the Garden

Enter HASTINGS

HASTINGS

What an idiot am I, to wait here for a fellow, who probably
takes a delight in mortifying me. He never intended to be
punctual, and I'll wait no longer. What do I see? It is he,
and perhaps with news of my Constance.

Enter TONY, *booted and spattered*

HASTINGS

My honest Squire! I now find you a man of your word.   5
This looks like friendship.

TONY

Ay, I'm your friend, and the best friend you have in the
world, if you knew but all. This riding by night, by the
bye, is cursedly tiresome. It has shook me worse than the
basket of a stage-coach.   10

HASTINGS

But how? Where did you leave your fellow travellers? Are
they in safety? Are they housed?

TONY

Five and twenty miles in two hours and a half is no such

bad driving. The poor beasts have smoked for it: rabbit
me, but I'd rather ride forty miles after a fox, than ten with   15
such varment.

HASTINGS

Well, but where have you left the ladies? I die with impatience.

TONY

Left them? Why where should I leave them, but where I
found them?   20

HASTINGS

This is a riddle.

TONY

Riddle me this then. What's that goes round the house, and
round the house, and never touches the house?

HASTINGS

I'm still astray.

TONY

Why that's it, mon. I have led them astray. By jingo,   25
there's not a pond or slough within five miles of the place
but they can tell the taste of.

HASTINGS

Ha! ha! ha! I understand; you took them in a round, while
they supposed themselves going forward. And so you have
at last brought them home again.   30

TONY

You shall hear. I first took them down Feather-bed Lane,
where we stuck fast in the mud. I then rattled them crack
over the stones of Up-and-down Hill—I then introduced
them to the gibbet on Heavy-tree Heath, and from that,
with a circumbendibus, I fairly lodged them in the horse-   35
pond at the bottom of the garden.

HASTINGS

But no accident, I hope.

TONY

No, no. Only mother is confoundedly frightened. She
thinks herself forty miles off. She's sick of the journey, and

---

14 *smoked* galloped at speed (1697)

14–15 *rabbit me* like 'drat me', a meaningless oath (1742)

16 *varment* vermin; hence, objectionable people (first usage). He is talking about
his mother and cousin

35 *circumbendibus* roundabout process (1681)

the cattle can scarce crawl. So if your own horses be ready,   40
you may whip off with cousin, and I'll be bound that no
soul here can budge a foot to follow you.

HASTINGS

My dear friend, how can I be grateful?

TONY

Ay, now it's dear friend, noble Squire. Just now, it was all
idiot, cub, and run me through the guts. Damn *your* way of   45
fighting, I say. After we take a knock in this part of the
country, we kiss and be friends. But if you had run me
through the guts, then I should be dead, and you might go
kiss the hangman.

HASTINGS

The rebuke is just. But I must hasten to relieve Miss   50
Neville; if you keep the old lady employed, I promise to
take care of the young one.   *Exit* HASTINGS

TONY

Never fear me. Here she comes. Vanish. She's got from the
pond, and draggled up to the waist like a mermaid.

Enter MRS HARDCASTLE

MRS HARDCASTLE

Oh, Tony, I'm killed. Shook. Battered to death. I shall   55
never survive it. That last jolt that laid us against the
quickset hedge has done my business.

TONY

Alack, mama, it was all your own fault. You would be for
running away by night, without knowing one inch of the
way.   60

MRS HARDCASTLE

I wish we were at home again. I never met so many
accidents in so short a journey. Drenched in the mud,
overturned in a ditch, stuck fast in a slough, jolted to a
jelly, and at last to lose our way. Whereabouts do you think
we are, Tony?   65

TONY

By my guess we should be upon Crack-skull Common,
about forty miles from home.

MRS HARDCASTLE

O lud! O lud! the most notorious spot in all the country.
We only want a robbery to make a complete night on't.

40 *cattle* stable slang for 'horses' (1680)
54 *draggled* dirtied by being dragged through wet mud (1513)
57 *quickset hedge* a hedge formed of 'quick'—i.e. living—plants (1535)

TONY

Don't be afraid, mama, don't be afraid. Two of the five   70
that kept here are hanged, and the other three may not find
us. Don't be afraid. Is that a man that's galloping behind
us? No; it's only a tree. Don't be afraid.

MRS HARDCASTLE

The fright will certainly kill me.

TONY

Do you see anything like a black hat moving behind the   75
thicket?

MRS HARDCASTLE

O death!

TONY

No, it's only a cow. Don't be afraid, mama; don't be afraid.

MRS HARDCASTLE

As I'm alive, Tony, I see a man coming towards us. Ah!
I'm sure on't. If he perceives us we are undone.   80

TONY (*Aside*)

Father-in-law, by all that's unlucky, come to take one of his
night walks. (*To her*) Ah, it's a highwayman, with pistols as
long as my arm. A damned ill-looking fellow.

MRS HARDCASTLE

Good heaven defend us! He approaches.

TONY

Do you hide yourself in that thicket, and leave me to   85
manage him. If there be any danger I'll cough and cry,
Hem! When I cough be sure to keep close.

     MRS HARDCASTLE *hides behind a tree in the Back Scene*

Enter HARDCASTLE

HARDCASTLE

I'm mistaken, or I heard voices of people in want of help.
Oh, Tony, is that you? I did not expect you so soon back.
Are your mother and her charge in safety?   90

TONY

Very safe, sir, at my aunt Pedigree's. Hem!

MRS HARDCASTLE (*From behind*)

Ah death! I find there's danger.

HARDCASTLE

Forty miles in three hours; sure, that's too much, my
youngster.

87 *keep close* stay hidden (1513)

---

87 s.d. *Back Scene* In fact Mrs Hardcastle would hide behind a tree formed by one
of the wings or side-scenes.

TONY
> Stout horses and willing minds make short journeys, as   95
> they say. Hem!

MRS HARDCASTLE (*From behind*)
> Sure he'll do the dear boy no harm.

HARDCASTLE
> But I heard a voice here; I should be glad to know from
> whence it came?

TONY
> It was I, sir, talking to myself, sir. I was saying that forty   100
> miles in four hours was very good going. Hem! As to be
> sure it was. Hem! I have got a sort of cold by being out in
> the air. We'll go in, if you please. Hem!

HARDCASTLE
> But if you talked to yourself, you did not answer yourself. I
> am certain I heard two voices, and am resolved (*Raising his*   105
> *voice*) to find the other out.

MRS HARDCASTLE (*From behind*)
> Oh! he's coming to find me out. Oh!

TONY
> What need you go, sir, if I tell you. Hem! I'll lay down my
> life for the truth—hem!—I'll tell you all, sir.
>> *Detaining him*

HARDCASTLE
> I tell you, I will not be detained. I insist on seeing. It's in   110
> vain to expect I'll believe you.

MRS HARDCASTLE (*Running forward from behind*)
> O lud, he'll murder my poor boy, my darling. Here, good
> gentleman, whet your rage upon me. Take my money, my
> life, but spare that young gentleman, spare my child, if you
> have any mercy.   115

HARDCASTLE
> My wife! as I'm a Christian. From whence can she come,
> or what does she mean!

MRS HARDCASTLE (*Kneeling*)
> Take compassion on us, good Mr Highwayman. Take our
> money, our watches, all we have, but spare our lives. We
> will never bring you to justice, indeed we won't, good Mr   120
> Highwayman.

HARDCASTLE
> I believe the woman's out of her senses. What, Dorothy,
> don't you know *me*?

MRS HARDCASTLE
> Mr Hardcastle, as I'm alive. My fears blinded me. But
> who, my dear, could have expected to meet you here, in   125

this frightful place, so far from home? What has brought
you to follow us?

HARDCASTLE

Sure, Dorothy, you have not lost your wits? So far from
home, when you are within forty yards of your own door?
(*To him*) This is one of your old tricks, you graceless rogue   130
you. (*To her*) Don't you know the gate, and the mulberry-
tree; and don't you remember the horse-pond, my dear?

MRS HARDCASTLE

Yes, I shall remember the horse-pond as long as I live; I
have caught my death in it. (*To* TONY) And it is to you, you
graceless varlet, I owe all this? I'll teach you to abuse your   135
mother, I will.

TONY

Ecod, mother, all the parish says you have spoiled me, and
so you may take the fruits on't.

MRS HARDCASTLE

I'll spoil you, I will.   *Follows him off the stage. Exeunt*

HARDCASTLE

There's morality, however, in his reply.   *Exit*   140

Enter HASTINGS *and* MISS NEVILLE

HASTINGS

My dear Constance, why will you deliberate thus? If we
delay a moment, all is lost for ever. Pluck up a little
resolution, and we shall soon be out of the reach of her
malignity.

MISS NEVILLE

I find it impossible. My spirits are so sunk with the agita-   145
tions I have suffered, that I am unable to face any new
danger. Two or three years' patience will at last crown us
with happiness.

HASTINGS

Such a tedious delay is worse than inconstancy. Let us fly,
my charmer. Let us date our happiness from this very   150
moment. Perish fortune. Love and content will increase
what we possess beyond a monarch's revenue. Let me
prevail.

MISS NEVILLE

No, Mr Hastings; no. Prudence once more comes to my
relief, and I will obey its dictates. In the moment of   155
passion, fortune may be despised, but it ever produces a
lasting repentance. I'm resolved to apply to Mr Hardcastle's compassion and justice for redress.

HASTINGS

But though he had the will, he has not the power to relieve
you.   160

MISS NEVILLE

But he has influence, and upon that I am resolved to rely.

HASTINGS

I have no hopes. But since you persist, I must reluctantly
obey you.   *Exeunt*

Act V, Scene iii

Enter SIR CHARLES *and* MISS HARDCASTLE

SIR CHARLES

What a situation am I in! If what you say appears, I shall
then find a guilty son. If what he says be true, I shall then
lose one that, of all others, I most wished for a daughter.

MISS HARDCASTLE

I am proud of your approbation, and to show I merit it, if
you place yourselves as I directed, you shall hear his   5
explicit declaration. But he comes.

SIR CHARLES

I'll to your father, and keep him to the appointment.

Exit SIR CHARLES

Enter MARLOW

MARLOW

Though prepared for setting out, I come once more to take
leave, nor did I, till this moment, know the pain I feel in
the separation.   10

MISS HARDCASTLE (*In her own natural manner*)

I believe those sufferings cannot be very great, sir, which
you can so easily remove. A day or two longer, perhaps,
might lessen your uneasiness, by showing the little value of
what you now think proper to regret.

MARLOW (*Aside*)

This girl every moment improves upon me. (*To her*) It   15
must not be, madam. I have already trifled too long with
my heart. My very pride begins to submit to my passion.
The disparity of education and fortune, the anger of a
parent, and the contempt of my equals, begin to lose their
weight; and nothing can restore me to myself, but this   20
painful effort of resolution.

11 *those* L (these 73)

MISS HARDCASTLE

Then go, sir. I'll urge nothing more to detain you. Though
my family be as good as hers you came down to visit, and
my education, I hope, not inferior, what are these advan-
tages without equal affluence? I must remain contented   25
with the slight approbation of imputed merit; I must have
only the mockery of your addresses, while all your serious
aims are fixed on fortune.

Enter HARDCASTLE *and* SIR CHARLES *from behind*

SIR CHARLES

Here, behind this screen.

HARDCASTLE

Ay, ay, make no noise. I'll engage my Kate covers him with   30
confusion at last.

MARLOW

By heavens, madam, fortune was ever my smallest consideration. Your beauty at first caught my eye; for who
could see that without emotion? But every moment that I
converse with you, steals in some new grace, heightens the   35
picture, and gives it stronger expression. What at first
seemed rustic plainness, now appears refined simplicity.
What seemed forward assurance, now strikes me as the
result of courageous innocence, and conscious virtue.

SIR CHARLES

What can it mean! He amazes me!   40

HARDCASTLE

I told you how it would be. Hush!

MARLOW

I am now determined to stay, madam, and I have too good
an opinion of my father's discernment, when he sees you,
to doubt his approbation.

MISS HARDCASTLE

No, Mr Marlow, I will not, cannot detain you. Do you   45
think I could suffer a connection, in which there is the
smallest room for repentance? Do you think I would take
the mean advantage of a transient passion, to load you with
confusion? Do you think I could ever relish that happiness,
which was acquired by lessening yours?   50

MARLOW

By all that's good, I can have no happiness but what's in
your power to grant me. Nor shall I ever feel repentance,

28 s.d. The two actors would enter from a stage door behind the projecting stage.

but in not having seen your merits before. I will stay, even   55
contrary to your wishes; and though you should persist to
shun me, I will make my respectful assiduities atone for the
levity of my past conduct.

MISS HARDCASTLE

Sir, I must entreat you'll desist. As our acquaintance
began, so let it end, in indifference. I might have given an
hour or two to levity; but seriously, Mr Marlow, do you
think I could ever submit to a connection, where *I* must   60
appear mercenary, and *you* imprudent? Do you think I
could ever catch at the confident addresses of a secure
admirer?

MARLOW (*Kneeling*)

Does this look like security? Does this look like confidence? No, madam, every moment that shows me your   65
merit, only serves to increase my diffidence and confusion.
Here let me continue——

SIR CHARLES

I can hold it no longer. Charles, Charles, how hast thou
deceived me! Is this your indifference, your uninteresting
conversation!   70

HARDCASTLE

Your cold contempt; your formal interview? What have
you to say now?

MARLOW

That I'm all amazement! What can it mean!

HARDCASTLE

It means that you can say and unsay things at pleasure.
That you can address a lady in private, and deny it in   75
public; that you have one story for us, and another for my
daughter.

MARLOW

Daughter!—this lady your daughter!

HARDCASTLE

Yes, sir, my only daughter. My Kate, whose else should
she be?   80

MARLOW

Oh, the devil.

MISS HARDCASTLE

Yes, sir, that very identical tall squinting lady you were
pleased to take me for (*Curtseying*). She that you addressed

---

56 *conduct* 73 (following this L has two speeches: Sr Chas I was never so confounded. Hard. I told you how it would be. Just now he'll deny every syllable of
this to our faces.)

as the mild, modest, sentimental man of gravity, and the
bold forward agreeable Rattle of the Ladies Club; ha! ha!   85
ha!

MARLOW
Zounds, there's no bearing this; it's worse than death.

MISS HARDCASTLE
In which of your characters, sir, will you give us leave to
address you? As the faltering gentleman, with looks on the
ground, that speaks just to be heard, and hates hypocrisy;   90
or the loud confident creature, that keeps it up with Mrs
Mantrap, and old Miss Biddy Buckskin, till three in the
morning; ha! ha! ha!

MARLOW
Oh, curse on my noisy head. I never attempted to be
impudent yet, that I was not taken down. I must be gone.   95

HARDCASTLE
By the hand of my body, but you shall not. I see it was all a
mistake, and I am rejoiced to find it. You shall not stir, I
tell you. I know she'll forgive you. Won't you forgive him,
Kate? We'll all forgive you. Take courage, man.

They retire, she tormenting him, to the Back Scene

Enter MRS HARDCASTLE, TONY

MRS HARDCASTLE
So, so, they're gone off. Let them go, I care not.   100

HARDCASTLE
Who gone?

MRS HARDCASTLE
My dutiful niece and her gentleman, Mr Hastings, from
Town. He who came down with our modest visitor here.

SIR CHARLES
Who, my honest George Hastings? As worthy a fellow as
lives, and the girl could not have made a more prudent   105
choice.

HARDCASTLE
Then, by the hand of my body, I'm proud of the connection.

MRS HARDCASTLE
Well, if he has taken away the lady, he has not taken her
fortune; that remains in this family to console us for her   110
loss.

87 *death* 73 (a charg'd culverin L)
90 *just to be heard* so as to be barely heard
97 *not stir* L (not, Sir 73)

HARDCASTLE

Sure Dorothy you would not be so mercenary?

MRS HARDCASTLE

Ay, that's my affair, not yours.

HARDCASTLE

But you know if your son, when of age, refuses to marry his cousin, her whole fortune is then at her own disposal. 115

MRS HARDCASTLE

Ay, but he's not of age, and she has not thought proper to wait for his refusal.

Enter HASTINGS *and* MISS NEVILLE

MRS HARDCASTLE (*Aside*)

What? returned so soon, I begin not to like it.

HASTINGS (*To* HARDCASTLE)

For my late attempt to fly off with your niece, let my present confusion be my punishment. We are now come 120 back, to appeal from your justice to your humanity. By her father's consent, I first paid her my addresses, and our passions were first founded in duty.

MISS NEVILLE

Since his death, I have been obliged to stoop to dissimulation to avoid oppression. In an hour of levity, I was ready 125 even to give up my fortune to secure my choice. But I'm now recovered from the delusion, and hope from your tenderness what is denied me from a nearer connection.

MRS HARDCASTLE

Pshaw, pshaw, this is all but the whining end of a modern novel. 130

HARDCASTLE

Be it what it will, I'm glad they're come back to reclaim their due. Come hither, Tony boy. Do you refuse this lady's hand whom I now offer you?

TONY

What signifies my refusing? You know I can't refuse her till I'm of age, father. 135

HARDCASTLE

While I thought concealing your age, boy, was likely to conduce to your improvement, I concurred with your mother's desire to keep it secret. But since I find she turns

114–15 HARDCASTLE. *But . . . disposal* L. In the printed editions, this speech is given to Mrs Hardcastle

116 s.p. MRS L (om. 73)

it to a wrong use, I must now declare, you have been of age
these last three months.   140

TONY

Of age! Am I of age, father?

HARDCASTLE

Above three months.

TONY

Then you'll see the first use I'll make of my liberty. (*Taking*
MISS NEVILLE*'s hand*) Witness all men by these presents,
that I, Anthony Lumpkin, Esquire, of BLANK place, refuse   145
you, Constantia Neville, spinster, of no place at all, for my
true and lawful wife. So Constance Neville may marry
whom she pleases, and Tony Lumpkin is his own man
again.

SIR CHARLES

O brave Squire.   150

HASTINGS

My worthy friend.

MRS HARDCASTLE

My undutiful offspring.

MARLOW

Joy, my dear George, I give you joy sincerely. And could I
prevail upon my little tyrant here to be less arbitrary, I
should be the happiest man alive, if you would return me   155
the favour.

HASTINGS (*To* MISS HARDCASTLE)

Come, madam, you are now driven to the very last scene of
all your contrivances. I know you like him, I'm sure he
loves you, and you must and shall have him.

HARDCASTLE (*Joining their hands*)

And I say so too. And Mr Marlow, if she makes as good a   160
wife as she has a daughter, I don't believe you'll ever repent
your bargain. So now to supper, tomorrow we shall gather
all the poor of the parish about us, and the Mistakes of the
Night shall be crowned with a merry morning; so, boy,
take her; and as you have been mistaken in the mistress,   165
my wish is, that you may never be mistaken in the wife.

EPILOGUE

By DR GOLDSMITH

Well, having stooped to conquer with success,
And gained a husband without aid from dress,
Still as a Barmaid, I could wish it too,
As I have conquered him to conquer you:
And let me say, for all your resolution,   5
That pretty Barmaids have done execution.
Our life is all a play, composed to please,
We have our exits and our entrances.
The first act shows the simple country maid,
Harmless and young, of every thing afraid;   10
Blushes when hired, and with unmeaning action,
'I hopes as how to give you satisfaction'.
Her second act displays a livelier scene.—
Th'unblushing Barmaid of a country inn.
Who whisks about the house, at market caters,   15
Talks loud, coquets the guests, and scolds the waiters.
Next the scene shifts to town, and there she soars,
The chop house toast of ogling connoisseurs.
On Squires and Cits she there displays her arts,
And on the gridiron broils her lovers' hearts—   20
And as she smiles, her triumphs to complete,
Even Common Councilmen forget to eat.
The fourth act shows her wedded to the Squire,

19 *Cit* 'a pert low townsman' (*SJ*; 1644)

EPILOGUE Goldsmith had considerable difficulty with the epilogue to *She Stoops to Conquer*. Joseph Cradock wrote an undistinguished piece, which was printed in 73 but not performed; it is not reproduced here. Arthur Murphy wrote another, which was also rejected. Goldsmith wrote three: firstly a 'quarrelling epilogue', to be spoken by Miss Catley and Mrs Bulkley, the actresses due to play Miss Neville and Kate. This was refused by the former, who then further refused to act in the play at all. He then wrote another, for Kate, which Colman, the manager, thought 'too bad to be spoken'; finally, at the last minute, this one, which was used in the production and printed at the beginning of 73. Goldsmith's two rejected epilogues are reproduced here in an appendix (pp. 97–101). .

8 *We have ... entrances* cf. *As You Like It*, II.iv, 43. The rest of the epilogue is a parody of Jaques's famous 'seven ages of man' speech.

And Madam now begins to hold it higher;
Pretends to taste, at Operas cries, *Caro*,   25
And quits her Nancy Dawson, for *Che faro*.
Dotes upon dancing, and in all her pride,
Swims round the room, the *Heinel* of Cheapside:
Ogles and leers with artificial skill,
Till having lost in age the power to kill,   30
She sits all night at cards, and ogles at spadille.
Such, through our lives, the eventful history—
The fifth and last act still remains for me.
The Barmaid now for your protection prays,
Turns Female Barrister, and pleads for Bayes.   35

25 *Caro* dear (Italian); hence, excellent, superb
31 *spadille* the name for 'the ace of spades at ombre' (*SJ*), a card game (1728)

26 *Nancy Dawson ... Che faro.* Nancy Dawson was a famous hornpipe dancer, who
   had a song named after her; 'che farò senza Euridice' the famous aria from Act
   III of Gluck's opera *Orfeo ed Euridice* (1762).
28 *Heinel.* Anna-Frederica Heinel, a famous dancer who appeared in the interludes
   that were a feature of the opera.
35 *Barrister ... Bayes.* Mr Bayes, the hero of Buckingham's *Rehearsal*, became a
   stock name for a dramatist; with a pun on 'bays', the laurel crown for poetry, and
   another, rather feeble one on barmaid/barrister.

APPENDIX

Song intended for
She Stoops to Conquer

Ah me, when shall I marry me?
Lovers are plenty but fail to relieve me;
He, fond youth, that could carry me,
Offers to love but means to deceive me.

But I will rally and combat the ruiner;   5
Not a look, not a smile shall my passion discover;
She that gives all to the false one pursuing her
Makes but a penitent, loses a lover.

SONG. James Boswell sent a copy of this pleasant, rather sentimental piece to the *London Magazine* of June 1774, with a letter: 'I send you a small production of the late Dr Goldsmith, which has never been published . . . he intended it as a song in the character of Miss Hardcastle . . . but it was left out, as Mrs Bulkeley, who played the part, did not sing'. Thus it was omitted from a late and finished version, and was definitely part of Goldsmith's final conception of his play, but it is hard to guess where it came from; perhaps it ended Act III, or followed Kate's speech in I.i, 151–7. Text from the autograph MS now at Yale.

First Rejected Epilogue for
She Stoops to Conquer

Enter MRS BULKLEY, *who curtseys very low as beginning to speak. Then enter* MISS CATLEY, *who stands full before her, and curtseys to the Audience*

MRS BULKLEY
Hold, ma'am, your pardon. What's your business here?
MISS CATLEY
The Epilogue.
MRS BULKLEY
The Epilogue?
MISS CATLEY
Yes, the Epilogue, my dear.
MRS BULKLEY
Sure you mistake, ma'am. The Epilogue, *I* bring it.   5
MISS CATLEY
Excuse me, ma'am. The Author bid *me* sing it.

RECITATIVE
Ye beaux and belles, that form this splendid ring,
Suspend your conversation while I sing.

MRS BULKLEY
Why sure the girl's beside herself: an Epilogue of singing.
A hopeful end indeed to such a blessed beginning.   10
Besides, a singer in a comic set!
Excuse me, ma'am, I know the etiquette.
MISS CATLEY
What if we leave it to the House?
MRS BULKLEY
The House!—Agreed.
MISS CATLEY
Agreed.   15
MRS BULKLEY
And she, who's party's largest, shall proceed.
And first I hope, you'll readily agree
I've all the critics and the wits for me.
They, I am sure, will answer my commands,
Ye candid judging few, hold up your hands;   20
What, no return? I find too late, I fear,
That modern judges seldom enter here.

Text from Goldsmith's *Works*, II (1801), 82–6

MISS CATLEY

    I'm for a different set.—Old men, whose trade is
    Still to gallant and dangle with the ladies.

RECITATIVE

    Who mump their passion, and who, grimly smiling,   25
    Still thus address the fair with voice beguiling.

AIR
Cotillon

    Turn, my fairest, turn, if ever
    Strephon caught thy ravished eye.
    Pity take on your swain so clever,
    Who without your aid must die.   30
      Yes, I shall die, hu, hu, hu, hu,
      Yes, I must die, ho, ho, ho, ho.

                        Da Capo

MRS BULKLEY

    Let all the old pay homage to your merit:
    Give me the young, the gay, the men of spirit.
    Ye travelled tribe, ye macaroni train   35
    Of French *friseurs* and nosegays justly vain,
    Who take a trip to Paris once a year
    To dress, and look like awkward Frenchmen here.
    Lend me your hands.—O fatal news to tell,
    Their hands are only lent to the Heinel.   40

MISS CATLEY

    Ay, take your travellers, travellers indeed!
    Give me my bonny Scot, that travels from the Tweed.
    Where are the Chiels? Ah! Ah, I well discern
    The smiling looks of each bewitching bairn.

AIR
A bonny young lad is my Jockey

    I'll sing to amuse you by night and by day,   45
    And be unco'merry when you are but gay;
    When you with your bagpipes are ready to play,
    My voice shall be ready to carol away
      With Sandy, and Sawney, and Jockey,
      With Sawney, and Jarvie, and Jockey.   50

---

24 *dangle S J* defines 'dangler' as 'a man that hangs about women only to waste time'.
    Perhaps here with a connotation of sexual impotence
25 *mump* 'to talk low and quick' (*S J*; 1586)
43 *Chiels* Scots dialect for 'children'

MRS BULKLEY

Ye Gamesters, who so eager in pursuit,
Make bust of all your fortune one *va toute:*
Ye Jockey tribe whose stock of words are few,
'I hold the odds.—Done, done, with you, with you'.
Ye Barristers, so fluent with grimace,   55
'My Lord,—your Lordship misconceives the case'.
Doctors, who cough and answer every misfortuner,
'I wish I'd been called in a little sooner',
Assist my cause with hands and voices hearty,
Come end the contest here, and aid my party.   60

AIR

Baleinamony

MISS CATLEY

Ye brave Irish lads, hark away to the crack,
Assist me, I pray, in this woeful attack;
For sure I don't wrong you, you seldom are slack,
When the ladies are calling, to blush, and hang back.
    For you're always polite and attentive,   65
    Still to amuse us inventive,
    And death is your only preventive.
      Your hands and your voices for me.

MRS BULKLEY

Well, madam, what if, after all this sparring,
We both agree, like friends, to end our jarring?   70

MISS CATLEY

And that our friendship may remain unbroken,
What if we leave the Epilogue unspoken?

MRS BULKLEY

Agreed.

MISS CATLEY

Agreed.

MRS BULKLEY

And now with late repentance,   75
Un-epilogued the Poet waits his sentence.
Condemn the stubborn fool who can't submit
To thrive by flattery, though he starves by wit.

          Exeunt

---

53 *Jockey* here meaning someone who has to do with horses—in any capacity (1638); previously, of course, meaning only a diminutive of 'Jock'

Second Rejected Epilogue for
She Stoops to Conquer

There is a place, so Ariosto sings,
A Treasury for lost and missing things.
Lost human wits have places there assigned them,
And they who lose their senses, there may find them,
But where's this place, this storehouse of the age?   5
The Moon, says he: but I affirm the Stage.
At least in many things I think I see
His lunar and our mimic world agree.
Both shine at night, for, but at Foote's alone,
We scarce exhibit till the sun goes down.   10
Both, prone to change, no settled limits fix,
'Tis said the folks of both are lunatics.
But in this parallel my best pretence is
That mortals visit both to find their senses.
To this strange spot, Rakes, Macaronis, Cits,   15
Come thronging to collect their scattered wits.
The gay Coquet, who ogles all the day,
Comes here by night, and goes a prude away.
The Gamester too, who, eager in pursuit,
Makes but of all his fortune one *va toute*,   20
Whose mind is barren, and whose words are few;
'I take the odds'—'Done, done, with you, and you',
Comes here to saunter, having made his bets,
Finds his lost senses out, and pays his debts.
The Mohawk too—with angry phrases stored   25
As 'damme sir', and 'sir, I wear a sword'—
Here lessoned for awhile, and hence retreating,
Goes out, affronts his man, and takes a beating.

23 *saunter* 'to loiter; to linger' (*SJ*; 1673)
25 *Mohawk* the Mohawks/Mohocks were aristocrats who amused themselves by
terrorizing people at night in the early eighteenth century (1711). Here used
metaphorically to express the readiness of the aristocracy to fight duels

Text from the MS now in the British Museum, probably in Mrs Bulkley's
handwriting (Add. MS 42515, ff. 83–4). Lines 9–10 and 29–42 are crossed out
in the MS. One can see why this long-winded and feeble poem was rejected.
1 *Ariosto* in his poem *Orlando Furioso* (XXXIV. 68ff.), followed by Pope at the end
of *The Rape of the Lock*, describes how all things lost on earth, including lost wits,
are stored on the moon.
9 *Foote's.* Samuel Foote in 1773 produced matinée puppet shows.

Here come the sons of scandal and of news,
But find no sense—for they had none to lose.   30
The poet too comes hither to be wiser,
And so for once I'll be the man's adviser.
What could he hope in this lord-loving age,
Without a brace of lords upon the stage,
In robes and stars unless the bard adorn us,   35
You grow familiar, lose respect, and scorn us.
Then not one passion, fury, sentiment
Sure his poetic fire is wholly spent!
Oh how I love to hear applauses shower
On my fixed attitude of half an hour.   40

Stands in an attitude

And then with whining, staring, struggling, slapping,
To force their feelings and provoke their clapping.
Hither the affected City Dame advancing,
Who sighs for operas, and dotes on dancing,
Who hums a favourite air, and spreading wide,   45
Swings round the room, the Heinel of Cheapside,
Taught by our art her ridicule to pause on,
Quits *Che faro* and calls for Nancy Dawson.
Of all the tribe here wanting an adviser
Our Author's the least likely to grow wiser;   50
Has he not seen how you your favours place
On Sentimental Queens, and Lords in lace?
Without a star, a coronet or garter,
How can the piece expect or hope for quarter?
No high-life scenes, no sentiment, the creature   55
Still stoops among the low to copy nature.
Yes, he's far gone. And yet some pity mix:
The English laws forbid to punish Lunatics.

33–40 *lord-loving ... attitude*. Goldsmith is again mocking Sentimental Comedy,
which, he thought, tended to depict the doings of the peerage, attitudinize, and
lack naturalism.